Also by James Michael Matthew:

Prophecy Before Vision
➤ American Writing Awards 2022
➤ New York Book Festival honorable mention 2022

Reject Self-Serving Power

BUILDING THE CLIMATE CHANGE BRIDGE

The Great Water Opportunity from Global Warming

JAMES MICHAEL MATTHEW

Archway Publishing books may be ordered through booksellers or by contacting:

Archway Publishing
1663 Liberty Drive
Bloomington, IN 47403
www.archwaypublishing.com
844-669-3957

Because of the dynamic nature of the Internet, any web addresses or links contained in this book may have changed since publication and may no longer be valid. The views expressed in this work are solely those of the author and do not necessarily reflect the views of the publisher, and the publisher hereby disclaims any responsibility for them.

Any people depicted in stock imagery provided by Getty Images are models, and such images are being used for illustrative purposes only.
Certain stock imagery © Getty Images.

ISBN: 978-1-6657-3430-1 (sc)
ISBN: 978-1-6657-3428-8 (hc)
ISBN: 978-1-6657-3429-5 (e)

Library of Congress Control Number: 2022922236

Print information available on the last page.

Archway Publishing rev. date: 12/08/2022

This book is dedicated to all the people around the world
who are struggling with understanding and deciding how best
to deal with global warming, climate change, rising ocean
coastlines, dwindling freshwater supplies, biodiversity loss, ocean
pollution, and desertification. This book sets forth solutions and
alternatives that can and will change and save the planet.

Net zero carbon was a great start. But it is time to move on and build the climate change bridge that will solve rising ocean coastlines, biodiversity loss, desertification, ocean pollution and depletion of freshwater supplies without destroying global economies along the way.
—James Michael Matthew

CONTENTS

ACKNOWLEDGMENTS

I want to acknowledge all the people who
I met while writing this book.

INTRODUCTION

Building the Climate Change Bridge is the first of a three-part series dedicated to providing new solutions for solving the critical problems brought by global warming, climate change, rising ocean coastlines, biodiversity loss, ocean pollution, desertification, and fresh water depletion. This book builds on chapter 21: Serendipity Pools for Climate Change, from my second book, *Reject Self-Serving Power.*[1]

Global warming and climate change are extremely difficult to understand and even harder to solve. Chapter 21 of my second book walks you through the history and literature background of climate change. As discussed therein, the primary problem with virtually all leadership to date is that there is no thought-through bridge for how to transition from a centuries-old society based on fossil fuels to a green-energy-based society.

Global warming is real. Climate change is real. Danger from rising global ocean coastlines is real. Biodiversity loss is real. Desertification is real. Depletion of ground and surface fresh water is real. Ocean pollution is real. But flying around in private jets to global conferences to espouse top-down ideology and issue alarm after alarm has not and will not set forth a viable transition plan or set of strategies and tactics that we can use to evolve from a society dependent on fossil fuels to a sustainable society.

This book was written to provide that transition—a bridge for how we can transition from fossil fuels to green-energy-based societies. A bridge for how we get there from here. As you read this book, you will come to appreciate that solving climate change is much more complicated than just carbon emissions and rising temperatures. This book focuses on the basic issues and offers solutions. My fourth book (the second of this series), *Defeating the New Axis Powers*, focuses on the geopolitical issues related to climate change. My fifth book (the third of this series), *The Two $20 Trillion Opportunities*, focuses on paying for climate change and preparing for *The Selfless Economy*. As you read my conclusions, solutions, and recommendations, please keep in mind that solving climate change will be all about making decisions under great uncertainty, among choices that often will seem unpalatable. Such is the case when confronting the challenges facing us.

1

Net-Zero Carbon—What It Is and What It Is Not

What It Is

ATTRIBUTES OF NET-ZERO carbon are summarized in the following list.

- Net-zero carbon is a concept advocating and promoting that all climate-change problems will be solved if we can reduce future net carbon emissions to zero through a combination of lowering future carbon emissions and removing past carbon emissions by an arbitrary date. That arbitrary date keeps getting extended, because the concept continues to flounder and fail. It is classic top-down ideology and dogma.
- It is a rallying cry and warning that climate change is real and must be addressed if humans and the planet are to survive.
- Net-zero carbon is a great start, but it is just a start.
- It is a false prophecy that if achieved, will stop rising temperatures, rising ocean coastlines, desertification, and biodiversity loss.

- Net-zero carbon is good intentions by honest and well-meaning professionals from around the world that have been hijacked by self-serving power zealots and politicians to promote themselves and increase their own power and wealth.

What It Is Not

What net-zero carbon is not is summarized in the following list.

- Net-zero carbon is not a thought-through set of strategies laying out a transition from fossil fuels to green energy. It assumes solar and wind power will serve as the world's main energy sources of the future. It assumes the end justifies the means—no matter the cost to generations in the interim.
- It is not a boots-on-the-ground, bottom-up driven, or capitalistic-filtered set of strategies and tactics that automatically sort themselves out in a capitalist-based economy.
- Net-zero carbon, even if and whenever achieved, will not stop rising ocean coastlines, biodiversity loss, desertification, ocean pollution, or fresh water depletion.
- It is not politically viable.
- Net-zero carbon is not sensitive to each individual country's energy and economic requirements.
- Nor is it sensitive to the unfairness of one or two generations bearing the cost and burden of unraveling climate-change sins from centuries of abuse.
- Net-zero carbon does not appreciate the complexity or unlikelihood of building the electric grid infrastructure necessary to convert from internal combustion engines to electronic vehicles (EVs).
- Net-zero carbon does not understand or consider the economics of global or country-by-country inflation caused by a war on fossil fuels.

The Three Pendulums of Energy Policy and Ideology

In my first book, *Prophecy before Vision*, we learned about the three pendulums of a society. Net-zero carbon is a textbook example of what happens when top-down ideology is followed in lieu of market-driven change. We are now seeing the three pendulums in action as free markets have engaged to correct net-zero carbon's over reach and missteps. Examples of pendulum swings include the following:

- Germany's retreat from its decades-old war on fossil fuels;
- New appreciation for nuclear power;
- The US Supreme Court's decision to slap down the EPA's crushing and unconstitutional regulations and war on fossil fuels;
- Political thrashing of fossil fuels warriors by the American electorate;
- Global inflation and economic chaos largely driven by the war on fossil fuels;
- "Ric Grenell to Newsmax: EU Definition of Green Energy Entirely Political";[2]
- "Biden's Green Energy Goals Shortsighted, Expert Says";[3]
- "The World War on Farmers";[4]
- "Protesting Dutch Farmers Reject Government's Terms for Dialogue";[5]
- "Kristi Noem to Newsmax: Those Who 'Control Our Food … Will Control Us";[6]
- "Fertilizer Industry and Farmer Advocates at Odds about Solutions to Fertilizer Crisis"; and[7]
- "A People's Revolt against Eco-Tyranny: From the Netherlands to Sri Lanka, People Have Had Enough of the Elite's Green Hysteria."[8]

2

Defeating the New Axis Powers

Axis Powers of the Past

EVERY FEW DECADES, dictators and self-serving narcissists from Europe, Asia, and the Middle East get together with the collective belief that they can conquer the free world and end democracy on the planet. The Axis powers in World War II were Germany, Italy, and Japan. Axis powers in World War I included Germany, Austria-Hungary, Bulgaria, and the Ottoman Empire. In the Crimean War, Russia fought against Britain, France, and the Ottoman Empire. In the end, democratic societies always won out, and the dictators lost.

The New Axis Powers

Unfortunately, here we go again. History is repeating itself with the new Axis powers forming. They believe that they have gotten it right this time and that a new world order has been formed—a world order where a few totalitarians at the top rule over everyone else. A new world order where their armies are beholden to the few totalitarians rather than the people of those nations. A new world order that weaponizes energy and other natural resources. This new world order would have no pendulums of society to correct their errors and bad ideas. Instead it would perpetuate linear thinking until it finally destroyed itself. For more information, read *Business Insider's* article "Putin Accused the US of Acting like God and Predicted a New World Order in Bullish St. Petersburg Speech" and *Quartz's* article "Chinese President Xi Jinping Has Vowed to Lead the 'New World Order.'"[9]

So what countries make up what I am calling the new Axis powers, and what are the criteria to be included? The criteria for inclusion are the desire to end the United States and its democratic allies and to have nuclear weapons. Therefore, the new Axis powers include China, Russia, Iran, and North Korea.

Friends of the New Axis Powers

The new Axis powers have a group of countries that support them and are not democracies, but they do not have nuclear weapons. I call this group the friends of the new Axis powers. These countries include Syria, Bulgaria, Cuba, Venezuela, and Nicaragua.

Unofficially Neutral Powers

There is a third group of countries that interestingly do not officially support the new Axis powers but do not hesitate to partner with them when it is convenient to do so. Countries that generally fall into this category include the following:

- Brazil;
- India;
- South Africa;
- Argentina;
- Indonesia; and
- others from time to time, depending on the topic.

Allies

As in the past, the Allies are comprised of the major democracies of the world. The current major countries include the members of NATO and European Union Countries, Japan, Australia, and South Korea.

Weaponizing Energy with Fossil Fuels at the Tip of the Spear

Why must we study and consider the new Axis powers when we study climate change and energy policy? The new Axis powers understand the importance of access to energy for a country and society to function. They hate the US and all democracies around the world. They believe their totalitarian forms of government will prevail in their self-envisioned new world order.

Global conflicts over energy are not new. Japan's attack on Pearl Harbor was about energy. But what differs this time around is the new Axis powers all have nuclear weapons. Unfortunately, the world is at a real risk of nuclear bombs being detonated. Global warming must take a back seat to defeating the new Axis powers.

I will go into much greater detail on this topic in my next book, but I included a chapter here because of the connections to energy policy. The geopolitics of energy policy cannot be denied and must be included in any strategy that has a remote hope of ultimate success. For more information, read *Fortune's* article "There's a Huge Problem for the Clean Energy Shift and It Comes from China, Unprecedented IEA Report Says."[10]

Russia's Invasion of Ukraine Has Changed Everything

Russia's invasion of Ukraine has opened the eyes of the world and laid bare the folly of net-zero carbon's attempt at globalization and top-down policy making. The invasion of Ukraine has also uncovered the true intentions of the new Axis powers—to control the world by destroying America and its allies. This is covered in the following four articles:

- "Russia Says the West Risks the 'Wrath' of God if It Punishes Moscow over War."[11]
- "'Doomsday' Submarine Armed with Nuclear Torpedoes Delivers to Russian Navy."[12]
- "How an Indian Cement Maker Bought Russian Coal Using Yuan."[13]
- "Russia-Ukraine Live News: Western Ministers Lambast Moscow at G20."[14]

My fourth book will go much more into depth on the topics in this chapter. You can also find further information in chapter 16 of my second book, *Why Are We Still Doing Business with China?*

3

Rising Ocean Coastlines

CHAPTER 21 OF my second book provides details on the background and current state of rising ocean coastlines. Our time here is best spent on analyzing and understanding the culprits driving the oceans' rising coastlines.

The oceans will continue to rise for centuries, even if net-zero carbon is achieved. Net-zero carbon is a goal that primarily targets temperatures in the atmosphere—the air outside of the oceans. Ocean levels are rising due primarily to three reasons.

First, warmer temperatures are melting historically frozen fresh and salt waters in cold regions of the world. This includes at the poles, in mountain glaciers, and in frozen grounds such as Greenland and Russia.

Second, water expands in volume as it increases in temperature; this process is called thermal expansion. Thermal expansion is due to the fact that cold water is denser than warm water. As ocean waters warm, the oceans expand in terms of cubic volume. Volume expansion then creates rising ocean levels, encroaching on coastlines around the world. Thermal expansion currently accounts for approximately 30 percent to 50 percent of rising ocean levels. This large disparity in estimate is due to differing satellite models accumulating information studied by different organizations. But even if you assume the lower level, it is a material reason for rising ocean levels. Warmer oceans also magnify the problem of reducing atmospheric temperatures, because oceans impact temperatures in the air. Historically, coastal temperatures have been cooled by the oceans. In both global warming and net-zero carbon scenarios, the opposite is true—warmer oceans will increase coastal and other atmospheric temperatures, even if net-zero carbon is achieved.[15]

The third and final reason is the depletion of fresh groundwaters and surface fresh waters. For millennium, long before the invention of the internal combustion engine, humans dug water wells, tapped lakes and rivers, and learned to irrigate crops. When underground water aquifers, springs, and other fresh waters are pumped to the surface and used, those waters eventually find their way into the oceans. Similarly, when rivers, lakes, and streams are accessed for use on land, those waters also eventually find their way into the oceans. Depletions of groundwaters and surface waters account for approximately 7 percent of rising ocean coastlines. Keep in mind, this 7 percent is a historical data point. Because cities, states, and regions are running out of fresh water, this number is likely increasing. How high will it go? Perhaps 10 percent or higher?

If we were to begin replacing depleted fresh waters, there could be a doubling effect on reducing rising ocean coastlines. A total run rate impact of 20 percent would not be unreasonable. The only time in modern history that ocean coastlines declined was during the era of global dam building. This history demonstrates that ocean coastlines can be lowered by keeping more water on land.

Groundwater Depletion Also Causes Sinking Lands

Groundwater depletion also leads to land sinking, especially around ocean coastlines.

As people pump water out of the ground, gaps form where the water used to be, causing the land to sink in order to fill the empty space. This leads to approximately 80% of the land sinkage in the US.[16]

The Battle to Beat Global Warming Is a Centuries-Long War, Not Years or Even Decades

The main takeaway from this chapter is that even *if* net-zero carbon is achieved by 2050, ocean coastlines will continue to rise for centuries thereafter due to thermal expansion and the depletion of land fresh waters. Atmosphere temperatures only account for approximately 50 percent of rising ocean levels. Furthermore, biodiversity loss, desertification, and the depletion of land fresh waters will not be stopped, even if net-zero carbon is achieved.

Extending the Main Runway

Winning the war against global warming is all about extending the war—extending the game. When the Japanese bombed Pearl Harbor, did Roosevelt and the US Navy go all in and invade Japan? No, they played it smart. They sent James Dolittle to let the Japanese know we were going to fight. When Russia invaded Eastern Ukraine, did the Ukraine Army stay and fight to the end? No, they played it smart. They inflicted great damage on Putin's murderers and cutthroats, but then they pulled back for the next fight. When you are in a basketball game and are clearly outmatched from the tipoff, do you try to throw a knockout punch in the first ten minutes? No, you just stay in and extend the game. Extend and win. The key to beating rising ocean coastlines is extending the game—extending the war—to give net-zero carbon enough time to ultimately win.

Building Off-Ramps

As you will see in the following chapters, net-zero carbon is wrongly credited as the answer to stopping biodiversity loss, desertification, and depletion of fresh land waters. While global warming certainly contributes to these problems, it is not the only culprit. Therefore, we need to not only extend the global warming runway but also build what I call off-ramps along the way to solve biodiversity loss, desertification, and depletion of fresh land waters.

4

Biodiversity Loss

What Is Biodiversity Loss?

ACCORDING TO THE *Encyclopedia Britannica,* the definition of biodiversity loss is a "reduction in the number of genes, individual organisms, species, and ecosystems in a given area."[17] The main causes of these areas of biodiversity loss include habitat loss, invasive species, over exploitation, pollution, and climate change associated with global warming.[18] As we can glean from this information, only approximately 20 percent of biodiversity loss is due to climate change associated with global warming.

For examples of biodiversity loss, read the article "Effort Begun to Eradicate Giant African Snails in Florida."[19] Also visit https://flpythonchallenge.org/ to learn about the Florida Python Challenge. "The Florida Python Challenge' is an exciting conservation effort which helps protect the rare Everglades habitat and the animals that live there from these invasive, nonnative snakes."[20]

Why Is Biodiversity Important?

In short, biodiversity provides us with clean air, fresh water, good quality soil and crop pollination. It helps us fight climate change and adapt to it as well reduce the impact of natural hazards. Since living organisms interact in dynamic ecosystems, the disappearance of one species can have a far-reaching impact on the food chain.[21]

Applying the use of serendipity pools—which we learned about in my first book—we can build off-ramps and use our war on rising ocean coastlines to solve biodiversity loss. For more information, see chapters 11, 12, and 13 and the article "Scientists Warn Deal to Save Biodiversity Is in Jeopardy."[22]

5

Desertification

SECOND ONLY TO the thermal expansion of the oceans, desertification is the least publicized but critical part of global warming to understand. For an in-depth education on desertification, you can read the IPCC report on the subject.[23] Here are some highlights:

> Desertification is land degradation in arid, semi-arid, and dry sub-humid areas, collectively known as drylands, resulting from many factors, including human activities and climatic variations. The range and intensity of desertification have increased in some dryland areas over the past several decades [high confidence]. Drylands currently cover about 46.2% [more or less 0.8%] of the global land area and are home to 3 billion people.

You can also read the Aspen Times's article "Recent Drop in Lake Powell's Storage Shows How Much Space Sediment Is Taking Up."[24]

The numbers listed in both are absolutely staggering. But what's even worse is they don't include most of the drylands that are depleting groundwaters and fresh waters. Clearly, depletion of freshwater supplies and the continued loss of livable lands is the most pressing matter related to global warming and climate change. For more information, read the articles "Top 10 Largest Deserts in the World by Total Area." and "Bill Gates' North Dakota Land Purchase Sparks Questions Online."[25] The latter discusses recent concern about billionaires buying up farmland as part of a green agenda. This pales in significance when compared to creating tens of millions of acres of new farmland through our plans, as set forth in the following chapters.

6

Thermal Expansion of the Oceans

THERMAL EXPANSION OF the oceans is the least understood but most important attribute of global warming in regards to rising ocean levels. Chapter 21 of my second book has a lengthy discussion and reference materials that you can access. That material is continued and enhanced in this chapter.

How Warming Water Causes Sea Level Rise

Sea level rise is caused by several different processes, including melting ice. But one big contributor to sea level rise is increasing global temperatures, which heat seas and cause something called thermal expansion of water. Thermal expansion happens when water gets warmer, which causes the volume of the water to increase. About half of the measured global sea level rise on Earth is from warming waters and thermal expansion.[26]

Thermal expansion happens when the ocean heats up. The heat causes sea water molecules to move slightly farther apart, taking up more space. The result is the ocean rises higher, flooding more land. Over the past several decades, about 40% of global sea level rise has been due to the effect of thermal expansion. The ocean, which covers about two-thirds of the Earth's surface, has been absorbing and storing more than 90% of the excess heat added to the climate system due to greenhouse gas emissions.[27]

The key takeaway for thermal expansion is that 90 percent of the excess heat added to the climate system is due to greenhouses. If net-zero carbon is ever achieved, it will still take centuries thereafter for the oceans to stop expanding while ocean waters mix and continue to heat themselves. Eventually, the oceans' temperatures will peak and then decline, followed by the land's temperatures. But that will take centuries, just as groundwater depletion has been going on for centuries. We need a runway to extend the game and win the centuries-long war on rising ocean coastlines.

7

Groundwater Depletion and Evaporating Freshwater Supplies

Groundwater Depletion

Groundwater is a valuable resource both in the United States and throughout the world. Where surface water, such as lakes and rivers, are scarce or inaccessible, groundwater supplies many of the hydrologic needs of people everywhere. In the United States, it is the source of drinking water for about half the total population and nearly all of the rural population, and it provides over 50 billion gallons per day for agricultural needs. Groundwater depletion, a term often defined as long-term water-level declines caused by sustained groundwater pumping, is a key issue associated with groundwater use. Many areas of the United States are experiencing groundwater depletion.

Excessive pumping can overdraw the groundwater "bank account". The water stored in the ground can be compared to money kept in a bank account. If you withdraw money at a faster rate than you deposit new money you will eventually start having account-supply problems. Pumping water out of the ground faster than it is replenished over the long-term causes similar problems. The volume of groundwater in storage is decreasing in many areas of the United States in response to pumping. Groundwater depletion is primarily caused by sustained groundwater pumping. Some of the negative effects of groundwater depletion:

- drying up of wells
- reduction of water in streams and lakes
- deterioration of water quality
- increased pumping costs
- land subsidence

What are some effects of groundwater depletion? Pumping groundwater at a faster rate than it can be recharged can have some negative effects of the environment and the people who make use of the water as discussed below:

LOWERING OF THE WATER TABLE

Pumping has removed water from storage in basalt aquifers and caused declines in many areas of the Columbia Plateau.

The most severe consequence of excessive groundwater pumping is that the water table, below which the ground is saturated with water, can be lowered. For water to be withdrawn from the ground, water must be pumped from a well that reaches below the water table. If groundwater levels decline too far, then the well owner might have to deepen the well, drill a new well, or, at least, attempt to lower the pump. Also, as water levels decline, the rate of water the well can yield may decline.

REDUCTION OF WATER IN STREAMS AND LAKES

There is more of an interaction between the water in lakes and rivers and groundwater than most people think. Some, and often a great deal, of the water flowing in rivers comes from seepage of groundwater into the streambed. Groundwater contributes to streams in most physiographic and climatic settings. The proportion of stream water that comes from groundwater inflow varies according to a region's geography, geology, and climate.

Groundwater pumping can alter how water moves between an aquifer and a stream, lake, or wetland by either intercepting groundwater flow that discharges into the surface-water body under natural conditions, or by increasing the rate of water movement from the surface-water body into an aquifer. A related effect of groundwater pumping is the lowering of groundwater levels below the depth that streamside or wetland vegetation needs to survive. The overall effect is a loss of riparian vegetation and wildlife habitat.

LAND SUBSIDENCE

The basic cause of land subsidence is a loss of support below ground. In other words, sometimes when water is taken out of the soil, the soil collapses, compacts, and drops. This depends on a number of factors, such as the type of soil and rock below the surface. Land subsidence is most often caused by human activities, mainly from the removal of subsurface water.

INCREASED COSTS FOR THE USER

As the depth to water increases, the water must be lifted higher to reach the land surface. If pumps are used to lift the water (as opposed to artesian wells), more energy is required to drive the pump. Using the well can become prohibitively expensive.

DETERIORATION OF WATER QUALITY

One water-quality threat to fresh groundwater supplies is contamination from saltwater intrusion. All of the water in the ground is not fresh water; much of the very deep groundwater and water below oceans is saline.

Where does groundwater depletion occur in the United States?

Groundwater depletion has been a concern in the Southwest and High Plains for many years, but increased demands on our groundwater resources have overstressed aquifers in many areas of the Nation, not just in arid regions. In addition, groundwater depletion occurs at scales ranging from a single well to aquifer systems underlying several states. The extents of the resulting effects depend on several factors including pumpage and natural discharge rates, physical properties of the aquifer, and natural and human-induced recharge rates. Some examples are given below.

ATLANTIC COASTAL PLAIN- In Nassau and Suffolk Counties, Long Island, New York, pumping water for domestic supply has lowered the water table, reduced or eliminated the base flow of streams, and has caused saline groundwater to move inland. Many other locations on the Atlantic coast are experiencing similar effects related to groundwater depletion. Surface-water flows have been reduced due to groundwater development in the Ipswich River basin, Massachusetts. Saltwater intrusion is occurring in coastal counties in New Jersey; Hilton Head Island, South Carolina; Brunswick and Savannah, Georgia; and Jacksonville and Miami, Florida (Barlow).

WEST-CENTRAL FLORIDA- Groundwater development in the Tampa-St. Petersburg area has led to saltwater intrusion and subsidence in the form of sinkhole development and concern about surface-water depletion from lakes in the area. In order to reduce its dependence on groundwater, Tampa has constructed a desalination plant to treat seawater for municipal supply.

GULF COASTAL PLAIN- Several areas in the Gulf Coastal Plain are experiencing effects related to groundwater depletion:

Groundwater pumping by Baton Rouge, Louisiana, increased more than tenfold between the 1930s and 1970, resulting in groundwater-level declines of approximately 200 feet.

In the Houston, Texas, area, extensive groundwater pumping to support economic and population growth has caused water-level declines of approximately 400 feet, resulting in extensive land-surface subsidence of up to 10 feet.

Continued pumping since the 1920s by many industrial and municipal users from the underlying Sparta aquifer have caused significant water-level declines in Arkansas, Louisiana, Mississippi, and Tennessee.

The Memphis, Tennessee area is one of the largest metropolitan areas in the world that relies exclusively on groundwater for municipal supply. Large withdrawals have caused regional water-level declines of up to 70 feet.

HIGH PLAINS- The High Plains aquifer (which includes the Ogallala aquifer) underlies parts of eight States and has been intensively developed for irrigation. Since predevelopment, water levels have declined more than 100 feet in some areas and the saturated thickness has been reduced by more than half in others.

PACIFIC NORTHWEST- Groundwater development of the Columbia River Basalt aquifer of Washington and Oregon for irrigation, public-supply, and industrial uses has caused water-level declines of more than 100 feet in several areas.

DESERT SOUTHWEST- Increased groundwater pumping to support population growth in south-central Arizona (including the Tucson and Phoenix areas) has resulted in water-level declines of between 300 and 500 feet in much of the area. Land subsidence was first noticed in the 1940s and subsequently as much as 12.5 feet of subsidence has been measured. Additionally, lowering of the water table has resulted in the loss of streamside vegetation.

Perennial streams, springs, and wetlands in the Southwestern United States are highly valued as a source of water for humans and for the plant and animal species they support. Development of ground-water resources since the late 1800's has resulted in the elimination or alteration of many perennial stream reaches, wetlands, and associated riparian ecosystems.

CHICAGO-MILWAUKEE AREA- Chicago has been using groundwater since at least 1864 and groundwater has been the sole source of drinking water for about 8.2 million people in the Great Lakes watershed. This long-term pumping has lowered groundwater levels by as much as 900 feet.[28]

Declining Surface Freshwater Supplies

Global warming is wreaking devastating effects on the rivers of the world. As both surface water supplies and groundwater supplies decline, their increased use and depletion of each other create a downward spiral of all freshwater supplies. Examples are as follows:

The Southwest is bone dry. Now, a key water source is at risk. Climate change and worsening drought have driven water stores to dangerous lows. Now the federal government is telling states to drastically cut back.

California and six other Western states have less than 60 days to pull off a seemingly impossible feat: Cut a multi-way deal to dramatically reduce their consumption of water from the dangerously low Colorado River.[29]

Great Salt Lake reaches new historic low. As the largest saltwater lake in the Western Hemisphere reached a new record low, the receding water levels in another lake exposed a relic that once sat nearly 200 feet below the surface.[30]

We're all struggling because there's no running water.[31]

There are communities on every continent running short of water, according to the United Nations. Desalination plants, which remove the salt from seawater, could help supply the fresh water needed. One radical solution could be using floating vessels equipped with desalination systems. Powered by nuclear reactors, these vessels could travel to islands, or coastlines, struck by drought, bringing with them both clean drinking water and power.[32]

SAN ANTONIO–Many South Texas rivers appear to be drying up during the current drought and heat wave.[33]

Water resources in the U.S. face a range of threats in a warming climate.[34]

For more information, you can use the following resources:

- "'Urgent Action Is Needed': Imperiled Great Salt Lake Drops to Historic Low"[35]
- "Great Salt Lake Is 'in Trouble' as Level Falls to Lowest on Record for Second Year in a Row"[36]
- "Po River–The Longest River in Italy–Dries Up"[37]
- "A Warming Climate Takes a Toll on the Vanishing Rio Grande"[38]

- "Dams and Taps Run Dry amid Historic Water Shortages in Northern Mexico"[39]
- "Water Levels at Lake Mead Dangerously Close to Hitting 'Dead Pool' Status"[40]
- "We Beg God for Water': Chilean Lake Turns to Desert, Sounding Climate Alarm"[41]
- "Low River Levels May Deepen Europe's Energy Crunch"[42]
- "Salt Lake City Confronts a Future without a Lake: Utah's Great Salt Lake Is Disappearing as a 'Megadrought' Persists across the Southwest, Forcing the Fast-Growing City nearby to Curb Its Water Use"[43]
- "History Lessons: Are Utahns 'Waking Up' to the Great Salt Lake's Peril?"[44]
- "As World Warms, Water Levels Dropping in Major Rivers"[45]
- "Freshwater Quality"[46]
- "Missouri River Drought Was Its Worst in 1,200 Years, Study Finds"[47]
- "Mississippi River Experiencing Low Water Levels Thanks to Lack of Rain in Northern Minnesota, Fueled by Climate Change"[48]
- "The Mississippi Embayment—Declining Water Levels in a Shallow Aquifer."[49]
- "Corn Belt Sees 'Rapid Onset of Drought'"[50]

Current Desalination Industry

Characteristics of the current desalination industry include the following:

> Desalination refers to a process that involves taking the salt out of water to make it drinkable. Desalination involves either treating sea or brackish water with the objective to create freshwater. In order to do this, desalination plants involve multiple technologies, from pre-treatment to pumps and membranes.

According to the new International Desalination Association (IDA) Water Security Handbook, the total global installed desalination capacity stands at 97.4 million cubic meters per day (m3/day) while the total global cumulative contracted capacity is 104.7 million m3/d.

As of June 30, 2018, more than 20,000 desalination plants had been contracted around the world. According to the International Water Association (IWA), desalination still only provides one per cent of the world's drinking water, but this is growing "year-on-year". The news in favor of desalination is that the world's oceans contain over 97.2 per cent of the planet's water resources, is "drought-proof and is practically limitless.[51]

8

Ocean Pollution

POLLUTION OF THE oceans has been widely publicized and known for years. The key point to consider regarding oceans' pollution is that while we build our strategy to combat global warming, we must include cleaning up the oceans. Major examples of the task before us include the following:

> While plastic debris is the most visible component of ocean pollution and is rapidly accumulating, it is the invisible chemicals, particles, metals, and biologic toxins that have been shown to affect human health. Ocean pollution poses a clear and present danger to human health and well-being, according to a new study from an international group of researchers. The study sounds the alarm that the growing global problem, which scientists are only beginning to understand, requires urgent and immediate action. It is a call to mobilize, say the authors who offer a path forward via pollution prevention and research recommendations.[52]

Eighty percent of pollution to the marine environment comes from the land. One of the biggest sources is called nonpoint source pollution, which occurs as a result of runoff. Nonpoint source pollution includes many small sources, like septic tanks, cars, trucks, and boats, plus larger sources, such as farms, ranches, and forest areas. Millions of motor vehicle engines drop small amounts of oil each day onto roads and parking lots. Much of this, too, makes its way to the sea.[53]

Ocean Pollution: 11 Facts You Need to Know

1. Ocean spills aren't the biggest problem.
2. More plastic than fish.
3. 5 garbage patches
4. Plastic poses a double danger.
5. China, Indonesia top the trash tally.
6. Pollution from laundry of synthetic clothes.
7. Most ocean trash sits on the bottom.
8. Even nutrients (agriculture) can become harmful.
9. The number of dead zones is growing.
10. The oceans are losing mussel mass.
11. Noise pollution carries in the waters.[54]

For more information, read the following articles:

- "Baltimore's 'Catastrophic Failures' at Wastewater Treatment Have Triggered a State Takeover, a Federal Lawsuit and Citizen Outrage"[55]
- "New Study Identifies Rapidly Emerging Threats to Oceans: The Push to Extract Materials and Food from the Oceans at Industrial Scale Menaces Vulnerable Communities and Biodiversity"[56]
- "Mining the Deep Sea for Battery Materials Will Be Dangerously Noisy, Study Finds: There Is a Looming Deadline to Address the Risk"[57]

9

Unsustainable Inflation and Energy Economics

THE PRIMARY FLAW of net-zero carbon is its blatant and elitist disregard for the resulting unsustainable inflation and destruction of country and global economies. This glaring weakness will unfortunately result in a bumpy ride for advocates of net-zero carbon. As the three pendulums of societies digest net-zero carbon, its weaknesses are exposed. Examples of these pendulum swings are outlined in the following:

- "The Unsustainable Costs of President Biden's Climate Agenda"[58]
- "Higher Energy Prices Cause Inflation Measures to Accelerate and Consumers to Reduce Real Consumption"[59]
- "Natural Gas Soars 700%, Becoming Driving Force in the New Cold War: Shortages of the Fuel Are Rippling throughout the Global Economy, Threatening Recessions and a Further Wave of Inflation"[60]

- "Consumers Are Hurting as 'Global Energy Shock' Gets Underway, Says World Energy Council"[61]
- "Energy Crisis Threatens Return of 1970s Inflation"[62]
- "Energy Crisis Causing Inflation Problem for Americans, National Security Threat: Mitch Roschelle"[63]
- "What Is the Relationship Between Oil Prices and Inflation?"[64]
- "The World May Be Careening toward a 1970s-Style Energy Crisis—or Worse"[65]
- "Outlooks for EU Growth and Inflation Worsen as Energy Crisis Hits"[66]
- "Why an Energy Crisis and $5 Gas Aren't Spurring a Green Revolution: As High Prices Move Consumers to Rethink Their Attachment to Oil and Gas, America Is Struggling to Meet the Moment"[67]
- "German Inflation Rate Hits Highest Level since 70s Oil Crisis"[68]
- "'The Situation Is More Than Dramatic': Germany Is Rationing Hot Water and Turning Off the Lights to Reduce Natural Gas Consumption"[69]
- "Energy Crisis: Causes and Consequences"[70]

10

Inter-Generational Obligations and Fairness

A GENERALLY ACCEPTED rule of climate change is that there is an implicit contract and responsibility for each generation to pass a healthy planet onto future generations. A weakness of net-zero carbon is that it expects the current generation to shoulder the climate sins of all past generations. This is not fair or doable.

> Intergenerational equity is a value concept which focuses on the rights of future generations. It is a notion that is implicit in ecological sustainability. However, since skills to facilitate thinking about long-term consequences are not typically included in educational curricula, this value is presented as distinct from ecological sustainability to emphasize the need for thinking about how human actions that directly or indirectly degrade the environment in the present will affect future generations of humans and other life

forms. Intergenerational equity is a notion that views the human community as a partnership among all generations. Each generation has the right to inherit the same diversity in natural and cultural resources enjoyed by previous generations and to equitable access to the use and benefits of these resources. At the same time, the present generation is a custodian of the planet for future generations, obliged to conserve this legacy so that future generations may also enjoy these same rights. In this way, intergenerational equity extends the scope of social justice into the future.[71]

What is fair is up to everyone to consider on their own. It is beyond the scope of our time here to define what is fair. Just be aware that this should be a consideration as we set our strategies to combat global warming and climate change.

The U.S. Supreme Court on Thursday dealt a major blow to the Environmental Protection Agency's power to regulate carbon emissions that cause climate change. The decision by the conservative court majority sets the stage for further limitations on the regulatory power of other agencies as well.[72]

For additional information, you can also read the articles "The EPA Prepares for Its 'Counterpunch' after the Supreme Court Ruling" and "U.S. Supreme Court Emissions Ruling May Stop SEC Drive for Disclosure."[73]

Shareholder activism by green energy advocates has been especially tortuous in recent years. In chapter 22 of my second book, I began my discussions on this topic before the US Supreme Court decision. In a future book, I will revisit this topic in more detail, especially considering the recent Supreme Court decision.

Green Energy Advocates' *Rubicon Circles of Power and Time*

In chapter 2 of my second book, we discussed the *Rubicon Circles of Power and Time,* which explains why all self-serving power strategies ultimately fail. Self-serving green energy politicians, bureaucrats, investors, and others have crossed their Rubicon circles. The rest of us have to unravel and fix the mess they got us into.

11

The End of Globalization

AT ITS CORE, net-zero carbon has always been a globalization-dependent strategy. Green energy advocates naively assumed that countries with very different energy needs, societies, and political goals would cooperate on their green energy agenda. Realities of geopolitics and energy-induced inflation have humbled the green energy agenda. Examples from around the World are as follows:

"The End of Globalization? What Russia's War in Ukraine Means for the World Economy"[74]

"The End of Globalization as We Know It"

> The tension between the unprecedented need for global collective action and a growing aspiration to rebuild political communities behind national borders is a defining challenge for today's policymakers. And it is currently unclear whether they can reconcile the two agendas.[75]

"Will the Ukraine War Spell the End of Globalization?"

> In a letter to shareholders last week, Larry Fink, the chief executive of BlackRock, the world's largest asset management company, issued a striking warning about a shift he perceived in the global economic order. Vladimir Putin's invasion of Ukraine had compelled governments and private companies like his own to retaliate by severing business ties with Russia."[76]

12

Conclusions, Solutions, and Recommendations

IN CHAPTER 21 of my second book, I set forth my calculations and research to come to the following conclusions, solutions, and recommendations.

- Number of Great Salt Lake equivalents required to utilize all cubic kilometers of water for rising ocean levels:
  - At Salt Lake depth: 4 meters: 35–138
  - Two times Salt Lake depth: 8 meters: 18–69
  - Four times Salt Lake depth: 16 meters: 9–35

Recommended Serendipity Pools and Climate Change Transition Pathways

After considering the numbers for the Great Salt Lake, the following recommendations form the foundation of our global climate change transition plan to build the climate change transition bridge.

- Create (dig) 25–100 Great Salt Lake equivalents (climate change lakes), using salt water from the oceans to fill them. Elements of such a transition plan would include the following.
    - Build salt water pipelines to pump and pipe salt water (preferably from dead zones) from the oceans to land-based climate change lakes. Presumably over time, the oceans should heal themselves as normal oxygenated waters fill in the removed dead zone waters.
    - Climate change lakes would be located in the deserts of the world, creating a massive increase in economic and environmental enhancements.
    - Use these separated climate change lakes to remediate the dead zones' oxygen-deficient ocean waters. Separating the dead zone waters into small batches would make it much easier to remediate the water than trying to remediate open ocean waters.
    - Use the climate change lakes to build fish stocks, which could be sent back into the oceans through the same pipelines in a two-way-flow system. Each climate change lake would also build its own land-based fishery economy.
    - Build desalination plants at each climate change lake to produce fresh water, which could be piped to replace depleted freshwater surface bodies and below ground aquifers, springs, etc. using a hub-and-spoke strategy and design.
    - Build floating and non-floating solar, nuclear, wind, hydroelectric and geothermal energy facilities next to the climate change lakes to power the desalination plants. Hydroelectric structures could be built both above and below waters and land, using natural and constructed steps.
    - Build additional desalination plants near ocean coasts not located in deserts to provide additional groundwater replacement supplies.

- o Eventually work with authorities to scale back the use of groundwaters, replacing them with desalinated water from climate change lakes. Assuming groundwaters are not used and are being replenished, this would approximate at least 15 percent (two times the current 7 percent depletion rate) of all rise in ocean coastlines.

- Build approximately 100–200 islands (climate change islands) around the world from current and future plastic and other debris in the oceans. Elements of such a transition plan could include the following.
  - o Build one hundred Galapagos-type islands and island groups with restricted access. Populate them with endangered species of all kinds. Starting with new islands that have no previous human inhabitants or owners will make it much easier to restrict them than would be the case for existing islands.
  - o Use the climate change islands as landfill depots where all countries of the world can ship their garbage and landfill. These landfill islands could develop specialties to remediate specific types of pollution.

The above solutions would also address the following four sustainable development goals (SDGs):

- SDG 6: clean water and sanitation,
- SDG 11: sustainable cities and communities,
- SDG 13: climate action, and
- SDG 15: life on land

Long-Term End Goals—Building the Permanent Infrastructure to Lower Ocean Levels, Filter Ocean Waters, and Replenish Depleted Freshwater Supplies

Increase the percentage of the fresh water on earth that is available for human use from 0.5 percent to 5.0 percent (a ten-fold increase). If this goal were achieved, it would theoretically imply that we could filter all the ocean waters every twenty years or so to filter out micro plastic fibers and other pollution.

13

Building the Climate Change Bridge

Primary Strategies to Build the Climate Change Bridge

TO BE VERY clear, our primary and foundational strategies for building the climate change bridge are to:

1. Transfer ocean salt waters to the deserts of the world in sufficient quantities to build a centuries-long runway to control rising ocean coastlines;
2. Desalinate those transferred salt waters to be used to reverse groundwater and surface fresh water depletion, ultimately increasing the world's usable and available fresh waters to 5 percent of the earth's total water; and
3. Use the infrastructure previously developed to reverse biodiversity loss, desertification, and ocean pollution.

Building the climate change bridge would include the following steps.

- Build and gain a consensus from federal, state, and local authorities for our plans set forth in this book, chapter 21 of my second book, and my white paper published on the JM Prophecies blog.
- Complete our network and team with partners, including those with expertise in construction, pipelines, desalination, marine biology, nuclear energy, solar energy, geothermal energy, aqua culture, desertification, biodiversity loss, groundwater depletion and replacement, and other areas to be determined in the early stages. For example:

  > Pipelines generate 55% of Enbridge earnings, gas transmission 40% and renewables 4%—changing that mix will costs billions.
  >
  > CALGARY–Enbridge Inc., North America's largest pipeline company, is shifting its asset mix to reflect the energy transition underway across the world.[77]

- Focus our initial projects on the Great Salt Lake and the Colorado River Basin.
- In the early stages, complete the following.
  - Calculate the amount of ocean waters that can be reasonably piped inland and the potential of this strategy slowing global rising ocean coastlines.
  - Demonstrate how retaining and storing fresh waters inland can remediate depleted groundwaters and other fresh waters as well as slow and remediate rising ocean coastlines.
  - Demonstrate how these strategies can be used to remediate biodiversity loss, stop desertification, and remediate polluted oceans.
  - Provide irrigation waters for areas not currently using irrigation but will need to do so in the future due to climate change.
- Assuming early stage results are favorable, build a chain of inland seas in North America. Under this plan, the states of Utah, Nevada, California, Arizona, Colorado, and New Mexico would

all have one inland sea dug in their deserts and desalination facilities built in their states. There would also be at least two additional inland seas dug and related desalination facilities built in northern Mexico.

o These projects could be used as learning and teaching centers for the rest of the World to emulate in other great deserts.

14

Paying for the Climate Change Bridge

CHAPTER 21 OF my second book sets forth the preliminary business model attributes to pay for the climate change bridge. Since the publication of my second book, we at JM Prophecies Corporation have continued to refine and expand our business model's recommendation on how to pay for the climate change bridge. I will publish my recommendations for how to pay for the climate change bridge in my fifth book, *The Two $20 Trillion Opportunities*.

15

Competitive Energy Technologies and Energy Diversification

THERE IS A wealth of alternative energy technologies being investigated and pursued around the world. As such, no one really knows what a long-term energy industry will look like or what the dominant technologies will be. Therefore, it is fascinating to me that depending on what builds their own self-serving power, people preach solar, wind, nuclear, geothermal, hydrogen, or something else as the source that will power the future. What is also fascinating is how so many politicians and bureaucrats are pushing the electric vehicle (EV) as our ultimate transportation industry at such an early stage. I have no idea what the winning technology or technologies will be. Most authors penning a book on energy policy would put technology near the front of their book. I place it near the end because I am technology indifferent. My plans do not rely on technology. All technology needed to implement my plans exist today. However, for what it is worth, my prophecy and contrarian mind is telling me the following:

- The demises of the internal combustion engine and fossil fuels are greatly exaggerated;
- The belief that EVs will become the dominant form of transportation is greatly exaggerated;
- Country-by-country energy security will dominate over globalization; and
- A smart energy policy would include at least ten different energy technologies, with no individual energy source providing more than 10 percent of a country's total energy plan.

For more information, you can read the article "When It Comes to Energy, Countries Should Mix It Up."[78]

16

The Great Water Opportunity from Global Warming

WINNING THE BATTLE against global warming is not about carbon emissions or net-zero carbon. It is not about technology. It is not about some arbitrary date that the World will end by if net zero carbon is not met. Winning the battle against global warming is all about water. Winning the battle against rising ocean coastlines is all about water. Winning the battles against biodiversity loss, desertification, groundwater and surface freshwater supplies depletion, and ocean pollution are all about water. Surpassing our obligations to future generations is all about water.

Global warming has provided us with the opportunity to increase usable and available fresh waters by several magnitudes. Rather than running around and doing our best Chicken Little imitations, we should embrace this historic opportunity to make the planet more environmentally healthy and compatible with human existence than it has been since before humans first walked on it.

Finally, I would argue depletion of our freshwater supplies is a much higher priority than rising ocean coastlines. If we lose the battle for ocean coastlines, we will have already lost the battle for adequate freshwater supplies. Everyone thinks people could just move inland to escape rising ocean coastlines. But if there is no fresh water, then where do we go? Flanked on one side by oceans and on the other by deserts.

17

Case Studies: Learning How to Build the Climate Change Bridge

THE CASE STUDIES presented in this chapter will help you learn how to build the climate change bridge.

Case Study 1: Net-Zero Carbon

Topic Introduction
Define and discuss your understanding of net-zero carbon.

Reader's Topic Analysis

____

Reader's Conclusions and Recommendations

____

Case Study 2: Climate Change Knowledge

Topic Introduction
Define and discuss your understanding of rising ocean coastlines.

Reader's Topic Analysis

Reader's Conclusions and Recommendations

Case Study 3: Climate Change Knowledge

Topic Introduction
Define and discuss your understanding of biodiversity loss.

Reader's Topic Analysis

Reader's Conclusions and Recommendations

Case Study 4: Climate Change Knowledge

Topic Introduction
Define and discuss your understanding of desertification.

Reader's Topic Analysis

Reader's Conclusions and Recommendations

Case Study 5: Climate Change Knowledge

Topic Introduction
Define and discuss your understanding of the thermal expansion of the oceans.

Reader's Topic Analysis

Reader's Conclusions and Recommendations

Case Study 6: Climate Change Knowledge

Topic Introduction
Define and discuss your understanding of groundwater and surface fresh water depletion.

Reader's Topic Analysis

Reader's Conclusions and Recommendations

Case Study 7: The Three Pendulums of Energy Policy and Ideology

Topic Introduction
Explain how the three pendulums of energy policy work and how they are changing the evolution of the green energy industry.

Reader's Topic Analysis

Reader's Conclusions and Recommendations

Case Study 8: The New Axis Powers

Topic Introduction

Do you agree with the author's assessment of what he has named the new Axis powers and their weaponization of energy? Why or why not?

Reader's Topic Analysis

Reader's Conclusions and Recommendations

Case Study 9: Russia's Invasion of Ukraine

Topic Introduction

Do you believe Russia's invasion of Ukraine has changed the green energy industry and movement? Why or why not?

Reader's Topic Analysis

Reader's Conclusions and Recommendations

Case Study 10: Desalination Industry

Topic Introduction

Define and discuss your understanding of the current state of the desalination industry.

Reader's Topic Analysis

Reader's Conclusions and Recommendations

Case Study 11: Ocean Pollution

Topic Introduction
What do you believe are the most important ocean pollutions to resolve, and why?

Reader's Topic Analysis

Reader's Conclusions and Recommendations

Case Study 12: Energy Economics

Topic Introduction
Discuss your understanding of how energy policy impacts inflation and global economies.

Reader's Topic Analysis

Reader's Conclusions and Recommendations

Case Study 13: Intergenerational Obligations and Fairness

Topic Introduction

Discuss what you believe are reasonable goals for your generation's obligations and environmental fairness to future generations.

Reader's Topic Analysis

Reader's Conclusions and Recommendations

Case Study 14: US Supreme Court Decision on EPA Regulations

Topic Introduction

Discuss your understanding of the Supreme Court's decision to restrict the Environmental Protection Agency's power to regulate carbon emissions that cause climate change.

Reader's Topic Analysis

Reader's Conclusions and Recommendations

Case Study 15: US Supreme Court Decision on EPA

Topic Introduction

What impact do you believe the Supreme Court's decision on EPA regulations will have on the Securities and Exchange Commission's rules for environmental disclosure and on other agencies such as the USDA?

Reader's Topic Analysis

Reader's Conclusions and Recommendations

Case Study 16: Green Energy Advocates' *Rubicon Circles of Power and Time*

Topic Introduction

Explain your understanding of the author's discussion on green energy advocates' *Rubicon Circles of Power and Time*. Do you agree with his assessment? Why or why not?

Reader's Topic Analysis

Reader's Conclusions and Recommendations

Case Study 17: Globalization

Topic Introduction

Discuss the role of globalization on green energy policy.

Reader's Topic Analysis

Reader's Conclusions and Recommendations

Case Study 18: Globalization

Topic Introduction

Do you agree with the author's belief that globalization is essentially dead? Why or why not?

Reader's Topic Analysis

Reader's Conclusions and Recommendations

Case Study 19: Conclusions, Solutions, and Recommendations

Topic Introduction
Read and discuss chapter 21 of *Reject Self-Serving Power*, specifically the author's calculations.

Reader's Topic Analysis

Reader's Conclusions and Recommendations

Case Study 20: Conclusions, Solutions, and Recommendations

Topic Introduction
Do you believe the author's conclusions, solutions, and recommendations are viable and reasonable enough to establish future climate change policy on? Why or why not?

Reader's Topic Analysis

Reader's Conclusions and Recommendations

Case Study 21: Conclusions, Solutions, and Recommendations

Topic Introduction

What enhancements or complete changes would you make to the author's plan?

Reader's Topic Analysis

Reader's Conclusions and Recommendations

**Case Study 22: Primary Strategies to Build
the Climate Change Bridge**

Topic Introduction

Do you agree with the author that there currently does not exist a plan that sets forth a reasonable solution to climate change or transition from fossil fuels to alternative energies? Why or why not?

Reader's Topic Analysis

Reader's Conclusions and Recommendations

**Case Study 23: Primary Strategies to Build
the Climate Change Bridge**

Topic Introduction

Discuss the author's three primary strategies to build the climate change bridge, as outlined in chapter 13. Include your agreement or disagreement on their viability.

Reader's Topic Analysis

Reader's Conclusions and Recommendations

Case Study 24: Paying for the Climate Change Bridge

Topic Introduction

Do you agree with the preliminary discussion regarding how to pay for the climate change bridge, as laid out in chapter 21 of the author's second book? Why or why not?

Reader's Topic Analysis

Reader's Conclusions and Recommendations

Case Study 25: Paying for the Climate Change Bridge

Topic Introduction

List and discuss how you would recommend paying for the climate change bridge.

Reader's Topic Analysis

Reader's Conclusions and Recommendations

Case Study 26: Competitive Energy Technologies and Energy Diversification

Topic Introduction

Do you agree with the author's discussion of competitive energy technologies and energy diversification? Why or why not?

Reader's Topic Analysis

Reader's Conclusions and Recommendations

Case Study 27: The Great Water Opportunity from Global Warming

Topic Introduction

Do you agree with the author's discussion on the great water opportunity from global warming? Why or why not?

Reader's Topic Analysis

Reader's Conclusions and Recommendations

NOTES

Chapter 1

- Net-zero carbon—what it is
- Net-zero carbon—what it is not
- The three pendulums of energy policy and ideology

Chapter 2

- Axis powers of the past
- The new Axis powers
- Friends of the new Axis powers
- Unofficially neutral powers
- Allies
- Weaponizing energy with fossil fuels at the tip of the spear
- Russia's invasion of Ukraine has changed everything

Chapter 3

- Chapter 21 of *Reject Self-Serving Power*
- Ocean levels are rising due primarily to three reasons
- The battle to beat global warming is a centuries-long war

- Extending the runway
- Building off-ramps

Chapter 4

- What is biodiversity loss?
- Why is biodiversity important?

Chapter 5

- Second only to the thermal expansion of the oceans, desertification is the least publicized but critical part of global warming to understand.
- Chapter 3 of IPCC's report

Chapter 6

- How warming waters cause sea level rise
- If net-zero carbon is ever achieved, it will still take centuries for the oceans to stop expanding.

Chapter 7

- Groundwater depletion
- Lowering the water table
- Reduction of water in streams and lakes
- Declining surface freshwater supplies
- Current desalination industry

Chapter 8

- While we build our strategy to combat global warming, we must include cleaning up the oceans.
- Most ocean pollution begins on land.
- Ocean pollution: eleven facts you need to know.

Chapter 9

- The primary flaw of net-zero carbon is its blatant and elitist disregard for the resulting unsustainable inflation and destruction of country and global economies.

Chapter 10

- A generally accepted rule of climate change is that there is an implicit contract and responsibility for each generation to pass a healthy planet onto future generations. A weakness of net-zero carbon is that it expects the current generation to shoulder the climate sins of all past generations. This is not fair or doable.
- What is fair is up to everyone to consider on their own.

Chapter 11

- At its core, net-zero carbon has always been a globalization-dependent strategy. Green energy advocates naively assumed countries with very different energy needs, societies, and political goals would cooperate on their green energy agenda. Realities of geopolitics and energy-induced inflation have humbled the green energy agenda.

Chapter 12

- Number of Great Salt Lake equivalents required to utilize all cubic kilometers of water for rising ocean levels:
    a. At Salt Lake depth: 4 meters: 35–138
    b. Two times Salt Lake depth: 8 meters: 18–69
    c. Four times Salt Lake depth: 16 meters: 9–35
- Recommended serendipity pools and climate change transition pathways
- Long-term end goal—building the infrastructure to filter all ocean waters

Chapter 13

- Primary strategies to build the climate change bridge
  - Our primary and foundational strategies to build the climate change bridge on are to:
    1. transfer ocean salt waters to the deserts of the world in sufficient quantities to build a centuries-long runway to control rising ocean coastlines;
    2. desalinate those transferred salt waters to be used to reverse groundwater and surface fresh water depletion, ultimately increasing the world's usable and available fresh waters to 5 percent of the earth's total water; and
    3. use the infrastructure previously developed to reverse biodiversity loss, desertification, and ocean pollution.
  - Focus our initial projects on the Great Salt Lake and the Colorado River Basin

Chapter 14

- Chapter 21 of *Reject Self-Serving Power* sets forth preliminary business model attributes to pay for the climate change bridge. Since the publication of my second book, we at JM Prophecies Corporation have continued to refine and expand our business model to develop recommendations on how to pay for the climate change bridge.

Preview

Defeating the New Axis Powers

SAME PLOT, NEW SCRIPT, NEW CAST, SAME ENDING

Defeating the New Axis Powers, my fourth book and the second of the Climate Change series, focuses on the geopolitical issues related to climate change.

Preview

The Two $20 Trillion Opportunities

PART 3 OF BUILDING THE CLIMATE CHANGE BRIDGE SERIES

PLANNING THE SELFLESS ECONOMY

FIXING OUR FINANCIAL MESS

The Two $20 Trillion Opportunities, my fifth book and the third of the Climate Change series, focuses on the 5 percent usable freshwater goal and *The Selfless Economy*

Preview

Learning Prophecy: 200 Case Studies to Learn Prophecy

CUMULATIVE CASE STUDIES WORKBOOK FROM BOOKS 1–5 AND NEW CASE STUDIES FOR CURRENT EVENTS

After my first five books are published, I plan to combine all case studies into a workbook. I will also add more case studies based on current events. These new case studies will use hindsight to see how well we forecasted our prophecies.

After the case study workbook is published, I will launch JM Prophecies Leadership and Decision Making Institute online. The case studies, my books, and recorded lectures will be the core materials for the institute. The case studies will also be published on our website to provide feedback and promote interaction.

Preview

The Leadership Broadcasting Company

A NEW ERA IN MEDIA, NEWS, AND INFORMATION TO CREATE TRUST AND REBUILD THE COUNTRY

The Leadership Broadcasting Company launches the JM Prophecies Corporation's media company.

Preview

Integrating the Economies of the Western Hemisphere

Integrating the Economies of the Western Hemisphere begins to build the serendipity pools and strategizes how we can finally integrate the economies of the Western Hemisphere for the advancement of all countries.

Preview

Crossing Waldo Road

BIRTHPLACE OF THE SELFLESS ECONOMY

Crossing Waldo Road will document our real-time activities to launch and establish the birthplace of *The Selfless Economy*.

Exhibits

Book 1 and Book 2
Case Studies

Exhibits for *Prophecy Before Vision*
Case Studies: Learning Prophecy

Case Study 1: Criminal Churn

Topic Introduction

The US criminal churn rate approximates seventeen times annually. This level of repeating offenders is over whelming our judicial system. As a result, judges, prosecutors, and politicians turn to ever-lenient prosecutorial strategies to lessen their caseloads. How can the churn rate best be reduced?

Reader's Topic Analysis

____

Reader's Conclusions and Recommendations

____

Case Study 2: Defunding the Police

Topic Introduction

Defunding the police is a topic of great debate. Using the data points presented in prior chapters, please argue both sides: yes, defund the police, or no, defunding the police is a detrimental concept and will only make matters worse.

Reader's Topic Analysis

____

Reader's Conclusions and Recommendations

____

Case Study 3: Mental Illness

Topic Introduction

During the past several years, the trend has been to close traditional mental health care hospitals and institutions. This trend has arguably led to massive numbers of cases where mental illness is not diagnosed or treated. Please provide your analysis of where the country lies as related to mental health care, and also provide any recommendations you may have.

Reader's Topic Analysis

Reader's Conclusions and Recommendations

Case Study 4: Drug Addiction

Topic Introduction

Imagine you are the parent of a twenty-year-old son. He started using drugs at the age of fifteen. Prior to that time, he was a great student, had many friends, and was admired by his younger brother and sister. He has now been a drug addict for five years. He dropped out of high school and has stolen from you many times to feed his addiction. He has been in and out of rehabilitation four times, each time coming out "clean" but slipping back into addiction. You still love your son, but you and his siblings can no longer believe he will ever get clean. In truth, knowing you all expect him to fail is part of his repeated failures.

Now imagine you are in front of the judge, hearing your son's case for stealing to feed his drug habit. The judge has just informed you of the facilities at JM Prophecies Brain Care. The judge asks your opinions regarding what sentence he should levy on your again convicted son. What would you recommend?

Reader's Topic Analysis

____

Reader's Conclusions and Recommendations

____

Case Study 5: Homelessness

Topic Introduction

You are a long-time owner of a beach-front house that you love. You paid $2 million for your house ten years ago. You had it appraised for refinancing two years ago and owe $4 million on a house that appraised for $6 million. An encampment of approximately 300 homeless people now surrounds your house, practically forcing you into staying inside. You no longer have access to the beach without walking through the encampment. A judge recently ruled that the local police can move the encampment but only if they can be moved to suitable housing.

Imagine your city council is meeting that very night, and you have been asked by your neighborhood watch group to testify. What would you say?

Reader's Topic Analysis

____

Reader's Conclusions and Recommendations

____

Case Study 6: Neighborhood Gangs Recruiting Your Children

Topic Introduction

Your son and daughter are both good high school students and never get into trouble. Over the last year, two competing criminal gangs have been recruiting both children to join their gangs or face dire consequences. Both gangs are also recruiting your younger elementary-school-aged children, further threatening your older children in their overall recruitment of all your children. The leaders of both gangs and most members were recently arrested and convicted of multiple crimes. The sentence hearing will be held next week, and the prosecutors have asked you to testify. What would you say?

Reader's Topic Analysis

Reader's Conclusions and Recommendations

Case Study 7: Prisoners' Futures

Topic Introduction

You have been in prison for ten years. You are up for parole. If paroled, you can leave the prison under oversight of a probation officer. You will have no job and nowhere to go. The parole board offers you the choice of staying in prison in one of JM Prophecies Brain Care's concentric villages of squares or going free onto the street. What would you ask for the board to clarify about JM Prophecies Brain Care, and what would you do?

Reader's Topic Analysis

Reader's Conclusions and Recommendations

Case Study 8: Prisoner's Family Members

Topic Introduction

You are the wife of a man currently in prison. He has been in prison for five years and has five more years to serve. His prison has entered into an agreement with JM Prophecies Brain Care. You and your children will have the opportunity to move into one of the JM Prophecies Brain Care's villages. What would you ask about JM Prophecies Brain Care, and what would you do?

Reader's Topic Analysis

Reader's Conclusions and Recommendations

Case Study 9: Entrepreneurs Relocating into a JM Prophecies Brain Care Village

Topic Introduction

You are an entrepreneur. You have identified a company you would like to purchase and become the CEO of, but you need external financing to complete the transaction. An affiliate of JM Prophecies has agreed to finance your acquisition with the requirement that you locate the company in a JM Prophecies set of concentric villages, which would place you and your employees next to a prison. What would you do?

Reader's Topic Analysis

Reader's Conclusions and Recommendations

Case Study 10: CEO Prophecy

Topic Introduction

You have read *Prophecy before Vision* and understand its power. What are your type I prophecies? What are your type II prophecies? How do you plan to publish your prophecies with your investors and board of directors? How will you articulate your updated vision to your employees?

Reader's Topic Analysis

Reader's Conclusions and Recommendations

Case Study 11: ESG Fund Manager

Topic Introduction

You have read *Prophecy before Vision* and understand its power. How will your Prophecies alter your investment strategies if at all?

Reader's Topic Analysis

Reader's Conclusions and Recommendations

Case Study 12: CEO—the Technologies of the Times

Topic Introduction

What do you consider to be the technologies of the times? How do you plan for them in your organization?

Reader's Topic Analysis

Reader's Conclusions and Recommendations

Case Study 13: CEO Prophecy—Three Pendulum Fissures

Topic Introduction

Do you believe there are any material fissures in the three pendulums
of a society that will impact your organization? If yes, what are they?

Reader's Topic Analysis

____

Reader's Conclusions and Recommendations

____

Case Study 14: CEO Prophecy—Serendipity Pools

Topic Introduction

You are the CEO of an international trading company. What serendipity
pools and strategy are you planning to recommend to your senior
management team?

Reader's Topic Analysis

____

Reader's Conclusions and Recommendations

____

Case Study 15: Marketing Senior Vice President—Prophecy

Topic Introduction

You have read _Prophecy before Vision_ and understand its power. Your
CEO has published his prophecies and has asked how do you look
at them from a marketing perspective? How will you articulate your
thoughts to your CEO?

Reader's Topic Analysis

____

Reader's Conclusions and Recommendations

____

Case Study 16: CEO and Board of Directors—Prophecy for China

Topic Introduction

At your collective strategy, decision, and direction, your Company has made a big bet investing in China. You obviously disagree with JM Prophecies' strategy and James Michael Matthew's first and fourth prophecies. Why do you disagree? What will happen to your company if you bet wrong?

Reader's Topic Analysis

____

Reader's Conclusions and Recommendations

____

Case Study 17: CEO and Board of Directors—Prophecy for Green Energy Economy

Topic Introduction

How do you see the conversion of an economy based on fossil fuel energy to one based on green energy playing out in the US and globally? What serendipity pools have you positioned for the coming of a green energy economy? What bets are you considering for pendulum swings created by the conversion? How are you positioning your company on the inside of the pendulum?

Reader's Topic Analysis

____

Reader's Conclusions and Recommendations

Case Study 18: CEO and Board of Directors—Prophecy—Aging Populations

Topic Introduction

Have you published any prophecies regarding the aging of populations? If yes, what are they and why did you pick them? If no, why not?

Reader's Topic Analysis

Reader's Conclusions and Recommendations

Case Study 19: CEO and Board of Directors—Prophecy—Studying and Analyzing Global Demographics

Topic Introduction

Does your company have an established methodology and forecasting policy for monitoring, analyzing, and forecasting global demographics? If no, why not? If yes, what are they? Do you maintain an actuarial chain-link historical forecasting model? If no, why not? If yes, how accurate has it been in predicting the future?

Reader's Topic Analysis

Reader's Conclusions and Recommendations

Case Study 20: CEO and Board of Directors—Prophecy—Things to Come

Topic Introduction

Have you published a list of "things to come" actions that you plan to take to alter the future? If yes, what are they? If no, why not? Do you believe you should reconsider?

Reader's Topic Analysis

____

Reader's Conclusions and Recommendations

____

Case Study 21: CEO and Board of Directors—Prophecy—Serendipity Pools

Topic Introduction

Have you ever discussed the concept of serendipity pools in any board meetings? If no, would you, or should you? Why or why not?

Reader's Topic Analysis

____

Reader's Conclusions and Recommendations

____

Case Study 22: CEO and Board of Directors—Prophecy—A Higher Power

Topic Introduction

Have you ever discussed the concept of a higher power in any board meetings? If no, would you, or should you? Why or why not?

Reader's Topic Analysis

____

Reader's Conclusions and Recommendations

____

Case Study 23: CEO and Board of Directors—Prophecy—Technologies of the Times

Topic Introduction

Have you published a list of the technologies of the times? If no, why not? If yes, what does the list look like?

Reader's Topic Analysis

____

Reader's Conclusions and Recommendations

____

Case Study 24: CEO and Board of Directors—Prophecy—Swings in the Civil Society Pendulum

Topic Introduction

Do you analyze and make predictions for the swings in the civil society pendulum? If no, why not? If yes, what would such a list of predictions look like?

Reader's Topic Analysis

____

Reader's Conclusions and Recommendations

____

Case Study 25: CEO and Board of Directors—*Prophecy before Vision*

Topic Introduction

After reading and studying *Prophecy before Vision*, do you believe it is possible for you to see and predict the future? Do you believe that there are "events to happen" as described in the book, that these events will happen, and that nothing can be done to change or prevent them? Do you believe that you can alter the future through the concept of "things to come"? Do you believe you and your people can always be the smartest people in the room? Do you believe you can make the right decision every time, with only 10 percent of the information? Do you believe there are signs from a higher power to guide you if you act for the good? For each of these questions, please explain why or why not. If you said yes, would you always have said yes?

Reader's Topic Analysis

Reader's Conclusions and Recommendations

Exhibits for *Reject Self-Serving Power Case Studies: Helping Others Be Successful*

Case Study 1: Doing Business in China

Topic Introduction

You are the chair of a publicly traded company that is listed and actively traded on a US stock exchange. You recently read a book documenting the scrutiny and legal and criminal liability incurred by large Japanese companies after World War II. You also read the one hundredth anniversary threat made to the world by the Chinese Communist Party. Your company recently made a large investment in China. What are you thinking, and what should you do? Would your answer change if China invaded Taiwan and/or launched a nuclear attack on Japan?

Reader's Topic Analysis

Reader's Conclusions and Recommendations

Case Study 2: Doing Business in China

Topic Introduction

Your CPA firm is the independent auditor of the company described in case study 1. You are the engagement partner. You have also read the same materials that the chair has read. What should you do? Has the company included any risk factors dealing with these potential issues in their SEC filings about their operations in China? If yes, what are they? If no, why not? Would your answer change if China invaded Taiwan and/or launched a nuclear attack on Japan?

Reader's Topic Analysis

____

Reader's Conclusions and Recommendations

____

Case Study 3: Doing Business in China

Topic Introduction

Your law firm is the lead SEC counsel for the company described in case study 1. You are the engagement partner. You have also read the same materials that the chair has read. What should you do? Has the company included any risk factors dealing with these potential issues in their SEC filings about their operations in China? If yes, what are they? If no, why not? Would your answer change if China invaded Taiwan and/or launched a nuclear attack on Japan?

Reader's Topic Analysis

____

Reader's Conclusions and Recommendations

____

Case Study 4: Target Markets at the Bottom of the Wealth Inequality Pyramid

Topic Introduction

You are the owner of a private company in the US. You have read both my first and second book. You are willing to assess whether these could be potential target markets for your company. Where do you begin your assessment?

Reader's Topic Analysis

Reader's Conclusions and Recommendations

Case Study 5: JM Prophecies Brain Care Corporation

Topic Introduction

You are the Governor of a state. Your state is suffering under a wave of crime. You are up for reelection and plan to run for another term. You have read my first and second book and are wondering if the proposals for both prison reform and clearing your state of crime could be viable solutions for you and your state. What should you do? How do you plan to make your initial assessments?

Reader's Topic Analysis

Reader's Conclusions and Recommendations

Case Study 6: JM Prophecies Brain Care Corporation

Topic Introduction

You are the attorney general of a state. Your state is suffering under a wave of crime. You are up for reelection and plan to run for another term. You have read my first and second book and are wondering if the proposals for both prison reform and clearing your state of crime could be viable solutions for you and your state. What should you do? How do you plan to make your initial assessments?

Reader's Topic Analysis

____

Reader's Conclusions and Recommendations

____

Case Study 7: JM Prophecies Brain Care Corporation

Topic Introduction

You are the warden of a large state prison. Your prison has a severe inmate aging issue. You have read both my first and second book. You are wondering if the proposal for prison reform as proposed by JM Prophecies Brain Care Corporation could be a viable solution for your prison. What should you do? How do you plan to make your initial assessments?

Reader's Topic Analysis

____

Reader's Conclusions and Recommendations

____

Case Study 8: JM Prophecies Leadership Code

Topic Introduction

You are the CEO of a publicly traded company. You have read the information and understand my discussions of the JM Prophecies leadership code. You are deciding if this leadership approach could be a fit for your company. What are your next steps?

Reader's Topic Analysis

____

Reader's Conclusions and Recommendations

Case Study 9: JM Prophecies Leadership Code

Topic Introduction

You are the managing partner of a large investment firm. You have read the information and understand my discussions of the JM Prophecies leadership code. You are deciding if this leadership approach could be a fit for your portfolio companies. What are your next steps?

Reader's Topic Analysis

Reader's Conclusions and Recommendations

Case Study 10: JM Prophecies Leadership Code

Topic Introduction

You are the founder and sole owner of a private manufacturing company. You have read the information and understand my discussions of the JM Prophecies leadership code. You disagree with my strategies for helping others be successful, instead believing you should make all the important decisions. You have a large bank loan, and the bank has asked if you are familiar with my works. What would you say?

Reader's Topic Analysis

Reader's Conclusions and Recommendations

Case Study 11: JM Prophecies Leadership Code

Topic Introduction

You are the banker of the company in case study 10. You have read the information and understand my discussions of the JM Prophecies leadership code. You agree with my strategies for helping others be successful, but the CEO and owner disagree. What would you say?

Reader's Topic Analysis

Reader's Conclusions and Recommendations

Case Study 12: Self-Serving Power

Topic Introduction

You are a member of a state legislature. Your family has had a long and successful political career. Your family has always operated with a ruthless, self-serving strategy. Your enemies have been plotting your family's demise. You have read *Reject Self-Serving Power* and want to have an open family discussion about your futures. What should you do and say?

Reader's Topic Analysis

Reader's Conclusions and Recommendations

Case Study 13: JM Prophecies Decision-Making Equation

Topic Introduction

Assume that the same circumstances as case study 12 are true here. What would your JM Prophecies decision-making equation look like?

Reader's Topic Analysis

Reader's Conclusions and Recommendations

Case Study 14: *Rubicon Circles of Power and Time*

Topic Introduction

Assume that the same circumstances as case study 12 are true here. How would you assess your Rubicon circles?

Reader's Topic Analysis

Reader's Conclusions and Recommendations

Case Study 15: Sea of Unforced Errors

Topic Introduction

Assume that the same circumstances as case study 12 are true here. What would your list of past mistakes, wrong decisions, and bad ideas for your family potentially look like? What would the list potentially look like for your enemies?

Reader's Topic Analysis

Reader's Conclusions and Recommendations

Case Study 16: Looking at Leadership through the Lens of the Bottom of the Wealth Inequality Pyramid

Topic Introduction

You are the CEO of a large private company. You have read my plea to look at these target market segments. What would you say and do?

Reader's Topic Analysis

Reader's Conclusions and Recommendations

Case Study 17: Looking at Leadership through the Lens of the Bottom of the Wealth Inequality Pyramid

Topic Introduction

You are the governor of a large state. You have read my plea to look at and study what JM Prophecies Brain Care Corporation is all about. You have also read my assertion that it is time to make our neighborhoods and country safe and to reform our outrageous prison system. You are currently assessing my claim that these two goals are *not* mutually exclusive and that we can solve both problems together at the same time. What are your assessments so far? What further questions do you have?

Reader's Topic Analysis

Reader's Conclusions and Recommendations

Case Study 18: Inequality Economics

Topic Introduction

You are on the staff of the Congressional Budget Office (CBO). You have read my proposal for inequality economics. What do you think?

Reader's Topic Analysis

Reader's Conclusions and Recommendations

Case Study 19: Reindustrialization of the US

Topic Introduction

You are the CEO of a large publicly traded manufacturing company based in the US. You have received an invitation from me to enter into a teaming agreement. What will you do?

Reader's Topic Analysis

Reader's Conclusions and Recommendations

Case Study 20: Circle of Life Retirement Strategy

Topic Introduction

You serve as an advisor to the social security board of trustees. You have read my recommendations for legislative changes to convert linear cliff retirement to a circle of life. What will you tell the board? What do you think they will say?

Reader's Topic Analysis

____

Reader's Conclusions and Recommendations

____

Case Study 21: Big Ideas, Quests, and Journeys

Topic Introduction

You serve on the board of a large think tank. You have read my chapter on big ideas, quests, and journeys. Do you have any ideas to bring to the pipeline? If yes, what are they?

Reader's Topic Analysis

____

Reader's Conclusions and Recommendations

____

Case Study 22: Integrating Western Hemisphere Economies

Topic Introduction

You are the president of a midsized Latin America Country. You have read my chapter on integrating western hemisphere economies. What are your thoughts?

Reader's Topic Analysis

____

Reader's Conclusions and Recommendations

____

Case Study 23: Reversing Time on the US Debt Clock

Topic Introduction

You are on the staff of a state governor, with responsibilities for assessing both your state's and the federal government's budget process. Have you historically used the US debt clock? If yes, how do you use it? If no, why not?

Reader's Topic Analysis

Reader's Conclusions and Recommendations

Case Study 24: It's Not about Race; It's about Leadership

Topic Introduction

You are an alderman for the city of Chicago. You have read my first two books and want to ask me to speak to the city council. What are the areas you want me to discuss?

Reader's Topic Analysis

Reader's Conclusions and Recommendations

Case Study 25: The Leadership Broadcasting Corporation

Topic Introduction

You are the CEO of a large media company. You have read the preview for my ninth book. What do you think?

Reader's Topic Analysis

Reader's Conclusions and Recommendations

REFERENCES

1   James Michael Matthew (Bloomington, IN: Archway Publishing, 2022), 118–137.

2   Luca Cacciatore, *Newsmax,* July 7, 2022, https://www.newsmax.com/newsmax-tv/newsmax-grenell-european-union-green-energy/2022/07/07/id/1077825/.

3   Michael Dorstewitz, *Newsmax,* July 6, 2022, https://www.newsmax.com/platinum/biden-green-energy-supreme-court/2022/07/06/id/1077499/.

4   John MacGhlionn, *Washington Times,* July 7, 2022, https://m.washingtontimes.com/news/2022/jul/7/the-worlds-war-on-farmers/.

5   Brady Knox, *Washington Examiner,* July 7, 2022, https://www.washingtonexaminer.com/news/protesting-dutch-farmers-reject-government-terms-dialogue.

6   Eric Mack, *Newsmax,* July 7, 2022, https://www.newsmax.com/newsmax-tv/kristi-noem-south-dakota-governor-2024/2022/07/07/id/1077826/.

7   Claire Carlson, *Successful Farming,* July 7, 2022, https://www.agriculture.com/news/business/fertilizer-industry-and-farmer-advocates-at-odds-about-solutions-to-fertilizer-crisis.

8   Brendan O'Neill, *Spiked,* July 6, 2022, https://www.spiked-online.com/2022/07/06/a-peoples-revolt-against-eco-tyranny/.

9   Bethany Dawson, "Putin Accused the US of Acting like God and Predicted a New World Order in Bullish St Petersburg Speech," *Business Insider,* June 18, 2022, https://www.businessinsider.com/putin-us-god-over-ukraine-crisis-new-world-order-coming-2022-6; Zheping Huang, "Chinese President Xi Jinping Has Vowed to Lead the 'New World Order,'" *Quartz,*

February 22, 2017, https://qz.com/916382/chinese-president-xi-jinping-has-vowed-to-lead-the-new-world-order/.

10   Yvonne Lau, *Fortune*, July 7, 2022, https://fortune.com/2022/07/07/iea-report-clean-energy-solar-transition-china-dominance/.

11   Holly Ellyatt, *CNBC*, July 7, 2022, https://www.cnbc.com/2022/07/07/russia-ukraine-live-updates.html.

12   Sam LaGrone, *USNI News*, July 8, 2022, https://news.usni.org/2022/07/08/doomsday-submarine-armed-with-nuclear-torpedoes-delivers-to-russian-navy.

13   Sudarshan Varadhan, Nupur Anand, and Aftab Ahmed, *Reuters*, July 8, 2022, https://www.reuters.com/markets/commodities/exclusive-how-an-indian-cement-maker-bought-russian-coal-using-yuan-2022-07-07/.

14   Sasha Petrova and Virginia Pietromarchi, *Aljazeera*, July 8, 2022, https://www.aljazeera.com/news/2022/7/8/ukraine-russia-live-news-donetsk-locals-brace-for-more-attacks-liveblog.

15   James Conca, "Climate Change Has the Earth in Hot Water," *Forbes*, August 31, 2015, https://www.forbes.com/sites/jamesconca/2015/08/31/climate-change-has-got-the-earth-in-hot-water/?sh=24704474d89e; "Understanding Climate: Physical Properties of Water" NASA, accessed June 8, 2022, https://sealevel.jpl.nasa.gov/ocean-observation/understanding-climate/air-and-water/; "IPCC Sixth Assessment Report: Impacts, Adaptation and Vulnerability," IPCC, accessed June 8, 2022, https://www.ipcc.ch/report/ar6/wg2/.

16   "Land Sinkage," Sea Level Rise.org, accessed July 6, 2022, https://sealevelrise.org/causes/.

17   *Encyclopedia Britannica Online*, s.v. "Primary Drivers of Biodiversity Loss," accessed June 8, 2022, https://www.britannica.com/study/learn-about-the-causes-of-biodiversity-loss.

18   *Encyclopedia Britannica Online*, s.v. "Biodiversity Loss."

19   Curt Anderson, *Yahoo News*, July 7, 2022, https://news.yahoo.com/effort-begun-eradicate-giant-african-175005623.html.

20   "Florida Python Challenge 2022," accessed July 7, 2022, https://flpythonchallenge.org/.

21   *European Parliament News*, "Biodiversity Loss: What Is Causing It and Why Is It a Concern?" September 6, 2021, https://www.europarl.europa.eu/news/en/headlines/society/20200109STO69929/biodiversity-loss-what-is-causing-it-and-why-is-it-a-concern.

22   Natasha Gilbert, *Nature*, June 30, 2022, https://www.nature.com/articles/d41586-022-01805-w.

23   "Chapter 3: Desertification," IPCC, accessed June 8, 2022, https://www.ipcc.ch/srccl/chapter/chapter-3/.

24   Laurine Lassalle, *Aspen Times*, July 9, 2022, https://www.aspentimes.com/news/recent-drop-in-lake-powells-storage-shows-how-much-space-sediment-is-taking-up/.

25   Zaraki Kenpachi, "Top 10 Largest Deserts in the World by Total Area," Red Rock Scenic Byway, June 12, 2022, https://devotedtonature.com/largest-deserts-in-the-world/; Jack Dutton, "Bill Gates' North Dakota Land Purchase Sparks Questions Online," *Newsweek*, July 7, 2022, https://www.newsweek.com/bill-gates-north-dakota-land-purchase-sparks-questions-online-1722660.

26   "How Warming Water Causes Sea Level Rise," Jet Propulsion Laboratory, accessed June 8, 2022, https://www.jpl.nasa.gov/edu/learn/project/how-warming-water-causes-sea-level-rise/#:~:text=Thermal%20expansion%20happens%20when%20water,warming%20waters%20and%20thermal%20expansion.

27   Jianjun Yin, "A New Report Predicts More Frequent, Destructive Flooding. What drives sea level rise?" *PBS*, February 17, 2022, https://www.pbs.org/newshour/science/a-new-report-predicts-more-frequent-destructive-flooding-what-drives-sea-level-rise.

28   Water Science School, "Groundwater Decline and Depletion," *USGS*, June 6, 2018, https://www.usgs.gov/special-topics/water-science-school/science/groundwater-decline-and-depletion.

29   Lara Korte, "The Southwest Is Bone Dry. Now, a Key Water Source Is at Risk," *Politico*, July 6, 2022, https://www.politico.com/news/2022/07/06/colorado-river-drought-california-arizona-00044121.

30   Adriana Navarro, "New Drone Footage Shows Dire State of the Great Salt Lake," *AccuWeather*, July 6, 2022, https://www.accuweather.com/en/climate/its-clear-the-lake-is-in-trouble-great-salt-lake-reaches-new-historic-low/1213231.

31   Laura Gottesdiener, "Dams, Taps Running Dry in Northern Mexico amid Historic Water Shortages," *Yahoo News,* June 20, 2022, https://news.yahoo.com/dams-taps-running-dry-northern-120215430.html.

32   Chris Baraniuk, "Could Nuclear Desalination Plants Beat Water Scarcity?" *BBC*, June 21, 2022, https://www.bbc.com/news/business-61483491.

33   RJ Marquez and Ken Huizar, "Zero flow? KSAT Visits Garner State Park to Get Firsthand Look at Frio River Conditions," *KSAT,* July 8, 2022, https://www.ksat.com/news/local/2022/07/08/zero-flow-ksat-visits-garner-state-park-to-get-firsthand-look-at-frio-river-conditions/.

34 "The Impact of Climate Change on Rivers," American Rivers, accessed July 8, 2022, https://www.americanrivers.org/threats-solutions/clean-water/impacts-rivers/.

35 Emilee Speck, *Fox Weather*, July 6, 2022, https://www.foxweather.com/weather-news/great-salt-lake-utah-drops-to-historic-low.

36 Rachel Ramirez, *CNN*, July 6, 2022, https://www.cnn.com/2022/07/06/us/great-salt-lake-record-low-climate/index.html.

37 European Space Agency, *SciTech Daily*, June 28, 2022, https://scitechdaily.com/po-river-the-longest-river-in-italy-dries-up/.

38 Jim Robbins, *Wired*, June 25, 2022, https://www.wired.com/story/a-warming-climate-takes-a-toll-on-the-vanishing-rio-grande/.

39 Daniel Becerril, *MSN*, March 3, 2022, https://www.msn.com/en-us/weather/topstories/lakes-and-rivers-dry-up-as-droughts-take-toll/ss-AAYNheR#image=1.

40 Julia Jacobo, *ABC News*, June 23, 2022, https://abcnews.go.com/US/water-levels-lake-mead-dangerously-close-hitting-dead/story?id=85584196.

41 Alexander Villegas and Rodrigo Gutierrez, *The Wire*, June 14, 2022, https://science.thewire.in/environment/penuelas-reservoir-13-year-drought-climate-crisis/.

42 Todd Gillespie, *gCaptain*, July 8, 2022, https://gcaptain.com/low-river-levels-may-deepen-europes-energy-crunch/.

43 Peter Yeung, *Bloomberg*, July 8, 2022, https://www.bloomberg.com/news/features/2022-07-08/drought-leaves-salt-lake-city-with-a-looming-water-crisis?utm_campaign=news&utm_medium=bd&utm_source=applenews.

44 Mark Shenefelt, *Globes*, June 15, 2022, https://www.globeslcc.com/2022/06/15/bonnie-baxter-great-salt-lake-microbiology-historical-perspective/.

45 National Science Foundation, *Science Daily*, April 22, 2009, https://www.sciencedaily.com/releases/2009/04/090421101625.htm.

46 EPA, Updated June 23, 2022, https://www.epa.gov/salish-sea/freshwater-quality.

47 Jordan Davidson, *EcoWatch*, May 12, 2020, https://www.ecowatch.com/missouri-river-drought-climate-crisis-2645979607.html.

48 Laura Schulte, *Milwaukee Journal Sentinel*, July 28, 2021, https://www.jsonline.com/story/news/local/wisconsin/2021/07/26/mississippi-river-low-water-levels-linked-climate-change/8012976002/.

49 USGS, December 2, 2010, https://www.usgs.gov/media/videos/mississippi-embayment-declining-water-levels-shallow-aquifer.

50 Chuck Abbott, *Successful Farming*, July 8, 2022, https://www.agriculture.com/news/business/corn-belt-sees-rapid-onset-of-drought.

51 "Desalination: Our Essential Guide to Desalination and the Global Water Crisis," Aqua Tech, October 2, 2019, https://www.aquatechtrade.com/news/desalination/desalination-essential-guide/.

52 Megan Avakian, "New Study Finds Ocean Pollution a Threat to Human Health," *NIH*, February 2021, https://www.niehs.nih.gov/research/programs/geh/geh_newsletter/2021/2/articles/new_study_finds_ocean_pollution_a_threat_to_human_health.cfm#:~:text=Ocean%20pollution%20is%20a%20complex%20mixture%20made%20up%20of%20mercury,mainly%20by%20eating%20contaminated%20seafood.

53 "What Is the Biggest Source of Pollution in the Ocean?" National Ocean Service, accessed June 14, 2022, https://oceanservice.noaa.gov/facts/pollution.html.

54 "Ocean Pollution: 11 Facts You Need to Know," Conservation, accessed June 14, 2022, https://www.conservation.org/stories/ocean-pollution-11-facts-you-need-to-know.

55 Aman Azhar, *Inside Climate News*, July 3, 2022, https://insideclimatenews.org/news/03072022/baltimore-wastewater/.

56 Rachel Rodriguez and Bob Berwyn, *Inside Climate News*, July 7, 2022, https://insideclimatenews.org/news/07072022/new-study-identifies-rapidly-emerging-threats-to-oceans/.

57 Justine Calma, *The Verge*, July 7, 2022, https://www.theverge.com/2022/7/7/23198447/mining-deep-sea-batteries-dangerously-noisy-study.

58 Kevin Dayaratna, Katie Tubb, and David Kreutzer, *Heritage*, June 16, 2022, https://www.heritage.org/energy-economics/report/the-unsustainable-costs-president-bidens-climate-agenda.

59 Fannie Mae, April 15, 2022, https://www.fanniemae.com/research-and-insights/forecast/higher-energy-prices-cause-inflation-measures-accelerate-and-consumers-reduce-real-consumption.

60 Gerson Freitas Jr., Stephen Stapcznyski, and Anna Shiryaevskya, *Bloomberg*, July 5, 2022, https://www.bloomberg.com/news/articles/2022-07-05/the-global-energy-crisis-just-got-even-worse-here-s-why.

61 Eustance Huang, *CNBC*, May 19, 2022, https://www.cnbc.com/2022/05/20/global-oil-crisis-and-inflation-hurt-consumers-world-energy-council.html.

62 Dan Eberhart, *Forbes*, October 19, 2021, https://www.forbes.com/sites/daneberhart/2021/10/19/energy-crisis-threatens-return-of-1970s-inflation/?sh=73308807e20f.

63 Talia Kaplan, *Fox News*, May 30, 2022, https://www.foxnews.com/media/energy-crisis-inflation-americans-national-security-threat-mitch-roschelle.

64 Nick Lioudis, *Investopedia*, May 5, 2022, https://www.investopedia.com/ask/answers/06/oilpricesinflation.asp.

65 Matt Egan, *CNN*, June 2, 2022, https://www.cnn.com/2022/06/02/business/energy-crisis-inflation/index.html.

66 Sam Fleming and Javier Espinoza, *Financial Times*, May 16, 2022, https://www.ft.com/content/cf9794ee-6b0d-4a50-a433-91cd76fab7a0.

67 Evan Halper, *Washington Post*, June 14, 2022, https://www.washingtonpost.com/business/2022/06/14/gas-prices-energy-climate/.

68 IANS, *Business Insider*, May 31, 2022, https://www.businessinsider.in/international/news/german-inflation-rate-hits-highest-level-since-70s-oil-crisis/articleshow/91911033.cms.

69 Tristan Bove, *Fortune*, July 8, 2022, https://fortune.com/2022/07/08/energy-rationing-germany-no-hot-water-turning-off-lights/.

70 Tom O'Keeffe, *Carraighill*, December 11, 2021, https://carraighill.com/european-energy-crisis-causes-and-consequences/.

71 J.K. Summers and L.M. Smith, "The Role of Social and Intergenerational Equity in Making Changes in Human Well-Being Sustainable," *Ambio* 43, no. 6 (October 2014): 718–728, https://www.ncbi.nlm.nih.gov/pmc/articles/PMC4165836/.

72 Nina Totenberg, "Supreme Court Restricts the EPA's Authority to Mandate Carbon Emissions Reductions," *NPR*, June 30, 2022, https://www.npr.org/2022/06/30/1103595898/supreme-court-epa-climate-change.

73 Juana Summers, Kat Lonsdorf, and Mallory Yu, "The EPA Prepares for Its 'Counterpunch' after the Supreme Court Ruling," *NPR*, July 1, 2022, https://www.npr.org/2022/07/01/1109486052/epa-supreme-court-emissions-target-ruling; Katanga Johnson, "U.S. Supreme Court Emissions Ruling May Stop SEC Drive for Disclosure," *Reuters*, July 1, 2022, https://www.reuters.com/business/sustainable-business/supreme-court-ruling-carbon-emissions-bodes-badly-us-sec-climate-rule-2022-06-30/.

74 Adam S. Posen, *Foreign Affairs*, March 17, 2022, https://www.foreignaffairs.com/articles/world/2022-03-17/end-globalization.

75 Jean Pisani-Ferry, Project Syndicate, June 28, 2021, https://www.project-syndicate.org/commentary/future-of-globalization-national-priorities-international-threats-by-jean-pisani-ferry-2021-06.

76 Spencer Bokat-Lindell, *New York Times*, March 30, 2022, https://www.nytimes.com/2022/03/30/opinion/ukrainne-russia-globalization-end.html.

77 Geoffrey Morgan, "North America's Largest Pipeline Company Aims to Pivot to Natural Gas and Renewable Energy," *Financial Post*, June 8, 2020, https://financialpost.com/commodities/energy/north-americas-largest-pipeline-company-aims-to-pivot-to-natural-gas-and-renewable-energy.

78 Mary-Katherine Ream, *Share America*, May 6, 2015, https://share.america.gov/diversifying-energy-sources-boosts-security/.

Abbott, Chuck. "Corn Belt Sees 'Rapid Onset of Drought.'" *Successful Farming*, July 8, 2022. https://www.agriculture.com/news/business/corn-belt-sees-rapid-onset-of-drought.

Ahmed, Aftab, Nupur Anand, and Sudarshan Varadhan. "How an Indian Cement Maker Bought Russian Coal Using Yuan." *Reuters*, July 8, 2022. https://www.reuters.com/markets/commodities/exclusive-how-an-indian-cement-maker-bought-russian-coal-using-yuan-2022-07-07/.

American Rivers. "The Impact of Climate Change on Rivers." Accessed July 8, 2022. https://www.americanrivers.org/threats-solutions/clean-water/impacts-rivers/.

Anderson, Curt. "Effort Begun to Eradicate Giant African Snails in Florida." *Yahoo News*, July 7, 2022. https://news.yahoo.com/effort-begun-eradicate-giant-african-175005623.html.

Aqua Tech. "Desalination: Our Essential Guide to Desalination and the Global Water Crisis." October 2, 2019. https://www.aquatechtrade.com/news/desalination/desalination-essential-guide/.

Avakian, Megan. "New Study Finds Ocean Pollution a Threat to Human Health." NIH. February 2021. https://www.niehs.nih.gov/research/programs/geh/geh_newsletter/2021/2/articles/new_study_finds_ocean_pollution_a_threat_to_human_health.cfm#:~:text=Ocean%20pollution%20is%20a%20complex%20

mixture%20made%20up%20of%20mercury,mainly%20by%20
eating%20contaminated%20seafood.

Azhar, Aman. "Baltimore's 'Catastrophic Failures' at Wastewater Treatment Have Triggered a State Takeover, a Federal Lawsuit and Citizen Outrage." *Inside Climate News*, July 3, 2022. https://insideclimatenews.org/news/03072022/baltimore-wastewater/.

Baraniuk, Chris. "Could Nuclear Desalination Plants Beat Water Scarcity?" *BBC*, June 21, 2022. https://www.bbc.com/news/business-61483491.

Becerril, Daniel. "Dams and Taps Run Dry amid Historic Water Shortages in Northern Mexico." *MSN*, March 3, 2022. https://www.msn.com/en-us/weather/topstories/lakes-and-rivers-dry-up-as-droughts-take-toll/ss-AAYNheR#image=1.

Berwyn, Bob, and Rachel Rodriguez. "New Study Identifies Rapidly Emerging Threats to Oceans." *Inside Climate News*, July 7, 2022. https://insideclimatenews.org/news/07072022/new-study-identifies-rapidly-emerging-threats-to-oceans/.

Bokat-Lindell, Spencer. "Will the Ukraine War Spell the End of Globalization?" *New York Times*, March 30, 2022. https://www.nytimes.com/2022/03/30/opinion/ukrainne-russia-globalization-end.html.

Bove, Tristan. "'The Situation Is More Than Dramatic': Germany Is Rationing Hot Water and Turning Off the Lights to Reduce Natural Gas Consumption." *Fortune*, July 8, 2022. https://fortune.com/2022/07/08/energy-rationing-germany-no-hot-water-turning-off-lights/.

Cacciatore, Luca. "Ric Grenell to Newsmax: EU Definition of Green Energy Entirely Political." *Newsmax*, July 7, 2022. https://www.newsmax.com/newsmax-tv/newsmax-grenell-european-union-green-energy/2022/07/07/id/1077825/.

Calma, Justine. "Mining the Deep Sea for Battery Materials Will Be Dangerously Noisy, Study Finds." *The Verge*, July 7, 2022. https://www.theverge.com/2022/7/7/23198447/mining-deep-sea-batteries-dangerously-noisy-study.

Carlson, Claire. "Fertilizer Industry and Farmer Advocates at Odds about Solutions to Fertilizer Crisis." *Successful Farming*, July 7, 2022. https://www.agriculture.com/news/business/fertilizer-industry-and-farmer-advocates-at-odds-about-solutions-to-fertilizer-crisis.

Conca, James. "Climate Change Has the Earth in Hot Water." *Forbes*, August 31, 2015. https://www.forbes.com/sites/jamesconca/2015/08/31/climate-change-has-got-the-earth-in-hot-water/?sh=24704474d89e.

Conservation. "Ocean Pollution: 11 Facts You Need to Know." Accessed June 14, 2022. https://www.conservation.org/stories/ocean-pollution-11-facts-you-need-to-know.

Davidson, Jordan. "Missouri River Drought Was Its Worst in 1,200 Years, Study Finds." *EcoWatch*, May 12, 2020. https://www.ecowatch.com/missouri-river-drought-climate-crisis-2645979607.html.

Dawson, Bethany. "Putin Accused the US of Acting like God and Predicted a New World Order in Bullish St Petersburg Speech." *Business Insider*, June 18, 2022, https://www.businessinsider.com/putin-us-god-over-ukraine-crisis-new-world-order-coming-2022-6.

Dayaratna, Kevin, David Kreutzer, and Katie Tubb. "The Unsustainable Costs of President Biden's Climate Agenda." *Heritage*, June 16, 2022. https://www.heritage.org/energy-economics/report/the-unsustainable-costs-president-bidens-climate-agenda.

Dorstewitz, Michael. "Biden's Green Energy Goals Shortsighted, Expert Says." *Newsmax*, July 6, 2022. https://www.newsmax.com/platinum/biden-green-energy-supreme-court/2022/07/06/id/1077499/.

Dutton, Jack. "Bill Gates' North Dakota Land Purchase Sparks Questions Online." *Newsweek*, July 7, 2022. https://www.newsweek.com/bill-gates-north-dakota-land-purchase-sparks-questions-online-1722660.

Eberhart, Dan. "Energy Crisis Threatens Return of 1970s Inflation." *Forbes*, October 19, 2021. https://www.forbes.com/sites/daneberhart/2021/10/19/energy-crisis-threatens-return-of-1970s-inflation/?sh=73308807e20f.

Egan, Matt. "The World May Be Careening toward a 1970s-Style Energy Crisis–or Worse." *CNN*, June 2, 2022. https://www.cnn.com/2022/06/02/business/energy-crisis-inflation/index.html.

Ellyatt, Holly. "Russia Says the West Risks the 'Wrath' of God if It Punishes Moscow over War." *CNBC*, July 7, 2022. https://www.cnbc.com/2022/07/07/russia-ukraine-live-updates.html.

EPA. "Freshwater Quality." Updated June 23, 2022, https://www.epa.gov/salish-sea/freshwater-quality.

Espinoza, Javier, and Sam Fleming. "Outlooks for EU Growth and Inflation Worsen as Energy Crisis Hits." *Financial Times*, May 16, 2022. https://www.ft.com/content/cf9794ee-6b0d-4a50-a433-91cd76fab7a0.

European Parliament News. "Biodiversity Loss: What Is Causing It and Why Is It a Concern?" September 6, 2021. https://www.europarl.europa.eu/news/en/headlines/society/20200109STO69929/biodiversity-loss-what-is-causing-it-and-why-is-it-a-concern.

European Space Agency. "Po River–the Longest River in Italy–Dries Up." *SciTech Daily*, June 28, 2022. https://scitechdaily.com/po-river-the-longest-river-in-italy-dries-up/.

Fannie Mae. "Higher Energy Prices Cause Inflation Measures to Accelerate and Consumers to Reduce Real Consumption." April 15, 2022. https://www.fanniemae.com/research-and-insights/forecast/higher-energy-prices-cause-inflation-measures-accelerate-and-consumers-reduce-real-consumption.

Florida Python Challenge. "Florida Python Challenge 2022." Accessed July 7, 2022. https://flpythonchallenge.org/.

Freitas, Gerson, Jr., Anna Shiryaevskya, and Stephen Stapcznyski. "Natural Gas Soars 700%, Becoming Driving Force in the New Cold War." *Bloomberg*, July 5, 2022. https://www.bloomberg.com/news/articles/2022-07-05/the-global-energy-crisis-just-got-even-worse-here-s-why.

Gilbert, Natasha. "Scientists Warn Deal to Save Biodiversity Is in Jeopardy." *Nature*, June 30, 2022. https://www.nature.com/articles/d41586-022-01805-w.

Gillespie, Todd. "Low River Levels May Deepen Europe's Energy Crunch." *gCaptain*, July 8, 2022. https://gcaptain.com/low-river-levels-may-deepen-europes-energy-crunch/.

Gottesdiener, Laura. "Dams, Taps Running Dry in Northern Mexico amid Historic Water Shortages." *Yahoo News*, June 20, 2022. https://news.yahoo.com/dams-taps-running-dry-northern-120215430.html.

Gutierrez, Rodrigo, and Alexander Villegas. "'We Beg God for Water': Chilean Lake Turns to Desert, Sounding Climate Alarm." *The Wire*, June 14, 2022. https://science.thewire.in/environment/penuelas-reservoir-13-year-drought-climate-crisis/.

Halper, Evan. "Why an Energy Crisis and $5 Gas Aren't Spurring a Green Revolution." *Washington Post*, June 14, 2022. https://www.washingtonpost.com/business/2022/06/14/gas-prices-energy-climate/.

Huang, Eustance. "Consumers Are Hurting as 'Global Energy Shock' Gets Underway, Says World Energy Council." *CNBC*, May 19, 2022. https://www.cnbc.com/2022/05/20/global-oil-crisis-and-inflation-hurt-consumers-world-energy-council.html.

Huang, Zheping. "Chinese President Xi Jinping Has Vowed to Lead the 'New World Order.'" *Quartz*, February 22, 2017. https://qz.com/916382/chinese-president-xi-jinping-has-vowed-to-lead-the-new-world-order/.

Huizar, Ken, and RJ Marquez. "Zero flow? KSAT Visits Garner State Park to Get Firsthand Look at Frio River Conditions." *KSAT*, July 8, 2022. https://www.ksat.com/news/local/2022/07/08/zero-flow-ksat-visits-garner-state-park-to-get-firsthand-look-at-frio-river-conditions/.

IANS. "German Inflation Rate Hits Highest Level since 70s Oil Crisis." *Business Insider*, May 31, 2022. https://www.businessinsider.in/international/news/german-inflation-rate-hits-highest-level-since-70s-oil-crisis/articleshow/91911033.cms.

IPCC. "Chapter 3: Desertification." Accessed June 8, 2022. https://www.ipcc.ch/srccl/chapter/chapter-3/.

IPCC. "IPCC Sixth Assessment Report: Impacts, Adaptation and Vulnerability." Accessed June 8, 2022. https://www.ipcc.ch/report/ar6/wg2/.

Jacobo, Julia. "Water Levels at Lake Mead Dangerously Close to Hitting 'Dead Pool' Status." *ABC News*, June 23, 2022. https://abcnews.go.com/US/water-levels-lake-mead-dangerously-close-hitting-dead/story?id=85584196.

Jet Propulsion Laboratory. "How Warming Water Causes Sea Level Rise." Accessed June 8, 2022. https://www.jpl.nasa.gov/edu/learn/project/how-warming-water-causes-sea-level-rise/#:~:text=Thermal%20expansion%20happens%20when%20water,warming%20waters%20and%20thermal%20expansion.

Johnson, Katanga. "U.S. Supreme Court Emissions Ruling May Stop SEC Drive for Disclosure." *Reuters*, July 1, 2022. https://www.reuters.com/business/sustainable-business/supreme-court-ruling-carbon-emissions-bodes-badly-us-sec-climate-rule-2022-06-30/.

Kaplan, Talia. "Energy Crisis Causing Inflation Problem for Americans, National Security Threat: Mitch Roschelle." *Fox News*, May 30, 2022. https://www.foxnews.com/media/energy-crisis-inflation-americans-national-security-threat-mitch-roschelle.

Kenpachi, Zaraki. "Top 10 Largest Deserts in the World by Total Area." Red Rock Scenic Byway, June 12, 2022. https://devotedtonature.com/largest-deserts-in-the-world/.

Knox, Brady. "Protesting Dutch Farmers Reject Government's Terms for Dialogue." *Washington Examiner*, July 7, 2022. https://www.washingtonexaminer.com/news/protesting-dutch-farmers-reject-government-terms-dialogue.

Korte, Lara. "The Southwest Is Bone Dry. Now, a Key Water Source Is at Risk." *Politico*, July 6, 2022. https://www.politico.com/news/2022/07/06/colorado-river-drought-california-arizona-00044121.

LaGrone, Sam. "'Doomsday' Submarine Armed with Nuclear Torpedoes Delivers to Russian Navy." *USNI News*, July 8, 2022. https://news.usni.org/2022/07/08/doomsday-submarine-armed-with-nuclear-torpedoes-delivers-to-russian-navy.

Lassalle, Laurine. "Recent Drop in Lake Powell's Storage Shows How Much Space Sediment Is Taking Up." *Aspen Times*, July 9, 2022. https://www.aspentimes.com/news/recent-drop-in-lake-powells-storage-shows-how-much-space-sediment-is-taking-up/.

Lau, Yvonne. "There's a Huge Problem for the Clean Energy Shift and It Comes from China, Unprecedented IEA Report Says." *Fortune*, July 7, 2022. https://fortune.com/2022/07/07/iea-report-clean-energy-solar-transition-china-dominance/.

Lioudis, Nick. "What Is the Relationship Between Oil Prices and Inflation?" *Investopedia*, May 5, 2022. https://www.investopedia.com/ask/answers/06/oilpricesinflation.asp.

Lonsdorf, Kat, Juana Summers, and Mallory Yu. "The EPA Prepares for Its 'Counterpunch' after the Supreme Court Ruling." *NPR*, July 1, 2022. https://www.npr.org/2022/07/01/1109486052/epa-supreme-court-emissions-target-ruling.

MacGhlionn, John. "The World War on Farmers." *Washington Times*, July 7, 2022. https://m.washingtontimes.com/news/2022/jul/7/the-worlds-war-on-farmers/.

Mack, Eric. "Kristi Noem to Newsmax: Those Who 'Control Our Food … Will Control Us." *Newsmax*, July 7, 2022. https://www.newsmax.com/newsmax-tv/kristi-noem-south-dakota-governor-2024/2022/07/07/id/1077826/.

Matthew, James Michael. *Reject Self-Serving Power.* Bloomington, IN: Archway Publishing, 2022.

Morgan, Geoffrey. "North America's Largest Pipeline Company Aims to Pivot to Natural Gas and Renewable Energy." *Financial Post*, June 8, 2020. https://financialpost.com/commodities/energy/north-americas-largest-pipeline-company-aims-to-pivot-to-natural-gas-and-renewable-energy.

NASA. "Understanding Climate: Physical Properties of Water." Accessed June 8, 2022. https://sealevel.jpl.nasa.gov/ocean-observation/understanding-climate/air-and-water/.

National Ocean Service. "What Is the Biggest Source of Pollution in the Ocean?" Accessed June 14, 2022. https://oceanservice.noaa.gov/facts/pollution.html.

National Science Foundation. "As World Warms, Water Levels Dropping in Major Rivers." *Science Daily*, April 22, 2009. https://www.sciencedaily.com/releases/2009/04/090421101625.htm.

Navarro, Adriana. "New Drone Footage Shows Dire State of the Great Salt Lake." *AccuWeather*, July 6, 2022. https://www.accuweather.com/en/climate/its-clear-the-lake-is-in-trouble-great-salt-lake-reaches-new-historic-low/1213231.

O'Keeffe, Tom. "Energy Crisis: Causes and Consequences." Carraighill. December 11, 2021. https://carraighill.com/european-energy-crisis-causes-and-consequences/.

O'Neill, Brendan. "A People's Revolt against Eco-Tyranny." *Spiked*, July 6, 2022. https://www.spiked-online.com/2022/07/06/a-peoples-revolt-against-eco-tyranny/.

Petrova, Sasha, and Virginia Pietromarchi. "Russia-Ukraine Live News: Western Ministers Lambast Moscow at G20." *Aljazeera*, July 8, 2022. https://www.aljazeera.com/news/2022/7/8/ukraine-russia-live-news-donetsk-locals-brace-for-more-attacks-liveblog.

Pisani-Ferry, Jean. "The End of Globalization as We Know It." Project Syndicate. June 28, 2021. https://www.project-syndicate.org/commentary/future-of-globalization-national-priorities-international-threats-by-jean-pisani-ferry-2021-06.

Posen, Adam S. "The End of Globalization? What Russia's War in Ukraine Means for the World Economy." *Foreign Affairs*, March 17, 2022. https://www.foreignaffairs.com/articles/world/2022-03-17/end-globalization.

Ramirez, Rachel. "Great Salt Lake Is 'in Trouble' as Level Falls to Lowest on Record for Second Year in a Row." *CNN*, July 6, 2022. https://www.cnn.com/2022/07/06/us/great-salt-lake-record-low-climate/index.html.

Ream, Mary-Katherine. "When It Comes to Energy, Countries Should Mix It Up." *Share America*, May 6, 2015. https://share.america.gov/diversifying-energy-sources-boosts-security/.Robbins, Jim. "A Warming Climate Takes a Toll on the Vanishing Rio Grande." *Wired*, June 25, 2022. https://www.wired.com/story/a-warming-climate-takes-a-toll-on-the-vanishing-rio-grande/.

Schulte, Laura. "Mississippi River Experiencing Low Water Levels Thanks to Lack of Rain in Northern Minnesota, Fueled by Climate Change." *Milwaukee Journal Sentinel*, July 28, 2021. https://www.

jsonline.com/story/news/local/wisconsin/2021/07/26/mississipp
i-river-low-water-levels-linked-climate-change/8012976002/.

Sea Level Rise.org. "Land Sinkage." Accessed July 6, 2022. https://
sealevelrise.org/causes/.

Shenefelt, Mark. "History Lessons: Are Utahns 'Waking Up' to
the Great Salt Lake's Peril?" *Globes*, June 15, 2022. https://
www.globeslcc.com/2022/06/15/bonnie-baxter-great-salt-lak
e-microbiology-historical-perspective/.

Smith, L.M., and J.K. Summers. "The Role of Social and Intergenerational
Equity in Making Changes in Human Well-Being Sustainable."
Ambio 43, no. 6 (October 2014): 718–728. https://www.ncbi.nlm.
nih.gov/pmc/articles/PMC4165836/.

Speck, Emilee. "'Urgent Action Is Needed': Imperiled Great Salt Lake Drops
to Historic Low." *Fox Weather*, July 6, 2022. https://www.foxweather.
com/weather-news/great-salt-lake-utah-drops-to-historic-low.

Totenberg, Nina. "Supreme Court Restricts the EPA's Authority to Mandate
Carbon Emissions Reductions." *NPR*, June 30, 2022. https://www.npr.
org/2022/06/30/1103595898/supreme-court-epa-climate-change.

USGS. "The Mississippi Embayment—Declining Water Levels in a Shallow
Aquifer." December 2, 2010. https://www.usgs.gov/media/videos/
mississippi-embayment-declining-water-levels-shallow-aquifer.

Water Science School. "Groundwater Decline and Depletion." USGS, June
6, 2018. https://www.usgs.gov/special-topics/water-science-school/
science/groundwater-decline-and-depletion.

Yeung, Peter. "Salt Lake City Confronts a Future without a
Lake." *Bloomberg*, July 8, 2022. https://www.bloomberg.
com/news/features/2022-07-08/drought-leaves-salt-lake-cit
y-with-a-looming-water-crisis?utm_campaign=news&utm_
medium=bd&utm_source=applenews.

Yin, Jianjun. "A New Report Predicts More Frequent, Destructive
Flooding. What drives sea level rise?" *PBS*, February 17, 2022.
https://www.pbs.org/newshour/science/a-new-report-predicts-more
-frequent-destructive-flooding-what-drives-sea-level-rise.